elevate science

SAVVAS
LEARNING COMPANY

You are an author!

This is your book to keep. Write and draw in it! Record your data and discoveries in it! You are an author of this book!

Print your name, school, town, and state below.

My Photo

Name

School

Town, State

Autobiography

SAVVAS
LEARNING COMPANY

ISBN-13: 978-0-134-98026-3
ISBN-10:   0-134-98026-3
4   20

Program Authors

ZIPPORAH MILLER, ED.D

Coordinator for K-12 Science Programs, Anne Arundel County Public Schools.
Zipporah Miller currently serves as the Senior Manager for Organizational Learning with the Anne Arundel County Public School System. Prior to that she served as the K-12 Coordinator for science in Anne Arundel County. She conducts national training to science stakeholders on the CA Next Generation Science Standards. Dr. Miller also served as the Associate Executive Director for Professional Development Programs and conferences at the National Science Teachers Association (NSTA) and served as a reviewer during the development of CA Next Generation Science Standards. Dr. Miller holds a doctoral degree from University of Maryland College Park, a master's degree in school administration and supervision from Bowie State University, and a bachelor's degree from Chadron State College.

MICHAEL J. PADILLA, Ph.D.

Professor Emeritus, Eugene P. Moore School of Education, Clemson University, Clemson, South Carolina
Michael J. Padilla taught science in middle and secondary schools, has more than 30 years of experience educating middle grades science teachers, and served as one of the writers of the 1996 U.S. National Science Education Standards. In recent years Mike has focused on teaching science to English Language Learners. His extensive leadership experience, serving as Principal Investigator on numerous National Science Foundation and U.S. Department of Education grants, resulted in more than $35 million in funding to improve science education. He served as president of the National Science Teachers Association, the world's largest science teaching organization, in 2005–2006.

MICHAEL E. WYSESSION, PH.D

Professor of Earth and Planetary Sciences, Washington University, St. Louis, Missouri
An author on more than 100 science and science education publications, Dr. Wysession was awarded the prestigious National Science Foundation Presidential Faculty Fellowship and Packard Foundation Fellowship for his research in geophysics, primarily focused on using seismic tomography to determine the forces driving plate tectonics. Dr. Wysession is also a leader in geoscience literacy and education, including being chair of the *Earth Science Literacy Principles*, author of several popular geology *Great Courses* video lecture series, and a lead writer of the *CA Next Generation Science Standards**.

Reviewers

Program Consultants

Carol Baker
Science Curriculum

Dr. Carol K. Baker is superintendent for Lyons Elementary K-8 School District in Lyons, Illinois. Prior to that, she was Director of Curriculum for Science and Music in Oak Lawn, Illinois. Before that she taught Physics and Earth Science for 18 years. In the recent past, Dr. Baker also wrote assessment questions for ACT (EXPLORE and PLAN), was elected president of the Illinois Science Teachers Association from 2011-2013 and served as a member of the Museum of Science and Industry advisory boards in Chicago. Dr. Baker received her BS in Physics and a science teaching certification. She is a writer of the Next Generation Science Standards. She completed her Master of Educational Administration (K-12) and earned her doctorate in Educational Leadership.

Jim Cummins
ELL

Dr. Cummins's research focuses on literacy development in multilingual schools and the role technology plays in learning across the curriculum. *Elevate Science* incorporates research-based principles for integrating language with the teaching of academic content based on Dr. Cummins's work.

Elfrieda Hiebert
Literacy

Dr. Hiebert is the President and CEO of TextProject, a nonprofit aimed at providing open-access resources for instruction of beginning and struggling readers, and a former primary school teacher. She is also a research associate at the University of California Santa Cruz. Her research addresses how fluency, vocabulary, and knowledge can be fostered through appropriate texts, and her contributions have been recognized through awards, such as the Oscar Causey Award for Outstanding Contributions to Reading Research (Literacy Research Association, 2015), Research to Practice Award (American Educational Research Association, 2013), William S. Gray Citation of Merit Award for Outstanding Contributions to Reading Research (International Reading Association, 2008).

Content Reviewers

Alex Blom, Ph.D.
Associate Professor
Department Of Physical Sciences
Alverno College
Milwaukee, Wisconsin

Joy Branlund, Ph.D.
Department of Physical Science
Southwestern Illinois College
Granite City, Illinois

Judy Calhoun
Associate Professor
Physical Sciences
Alverno College
Milwaukee, Wisconsin

Stefan Debbert
Associate Professor of Chemistry
Lawrence University
Appleton, Wisconsin

Diane Doser
Professor
Department of Geological Sciences
University of Texas at El Paso
El Paso, Texas

Rick Duhrkopf, Ph. D.
Department of Biology
Baylor University
Waco, Texas

Jennifer Liang
University Of Minnesota Duluth
Duluth, Minnesota

Heather Mernitz, Ph.D.
Associate Professor of Physical Sciences
Alverno College
Milwaukee, Wisconsin

Joseph McCullough, Ph.D.
Cabrillo College
Aptos, California

Katie M. Nemeth, Ph.D.
Assistant Professor
College of Science and Engineering
University of Minnesota Duluth
Duluth, Minnesota

Maik Pertermann
Department of Geology
Western Wyoming Community College
Rock Springs, Wyoming

Scott Rochette
Department of the Earth Sciences
The College at Brockport
State University of New York
Brockport, New York

David Schuster
Washington University in St Louis
St. Louis, Missouri

Shannon Stevenson
Department of Biology
University of Minnesota Duluth
Duluth, Minnesota

Paul Stoddard, Ph.D.
Department of Geology and Environmental Geosciences
Northern Illinois University
DeKalb, Illinois

Nancy Taylor
American Public University
Charles Town, West Virginia

Safety Reviewers

Douglas Mandt, M.S.
Science Education Consultant
Edgewood, Washington

Juliana Textley, Ph.D.
Author, NSTA books on school science safety
Adjunct Professor
Lesley University
Cambridge, Massachusetts

Teacher Reviewers

Rita Armstrong
Los Cerritos Middle School
Thousand Oaks, California

Tyler C. Britt, Ed.S.
Curriculum & Instructional
Practice Coordinator
Raytown Quality Schools
Raytown, Missouri

Holly Bowser
Barstow High School
Barstow, California

David Budai
Coachella Valley Unified School District
Coachella, California

A. Colleen Campos
Grandview High School
Aurora, Colorado

Jodi DeRoos
Mojave River Academy
Colton, California

Colleen Duncan
Moore Middle School
Redlands, California

Nicole Hawke
Westside Elementary
Thermal, California

Margaret Henry
Lebanon Junior High School
Lebanon, Ohio

Ashley Humphrey
Riverside Preparatory Elementary
Oro Grande, California

Adrianne Kilzer
Riverside Preparatory Elementary
Oro Grande, California

Danielle King
Barstow Unified School District
Barstow, California

Kathryn Kooyman
Riverside Preparatory Elementary
Oro Grande, California

Esther Leonard M.Ed. and L.M.T.
Gifted and Talented Implementation Specialist
San Antonio Independent School District
San Antonio, Texas

Diana M. Maiorca, M.Ed.
Los Cerritos Middle School
Thousand Oaks, California

Kevin J. Maser, Ed.D.
H. Frank Carey Jr/Sr High School
Franklin Square, New York

Corey Mayle
Brogden Middle School
Durham, North Carolina

Keith McCarthy
George Washington Middle School
Wayne, New Jersey

Rudolph Patterson
Cobalt Institute of Math and Science
Victorville, California

Yolanda O. Peña
John F. Kennedy Junior High School
West Valley City, Utah

Stacey Phelps
Mojave River Academy
Oro Grande, California

Susan Pierce
Bryn Mawr Elementary
Redlands Unified School District
Redlands, California

Cristina Ramos
Mentone Elementary School
Redlands Unified School District
Mentone, California

Mary Regis
Franklin Elementary School
Redlands, California

Bryna Selig
Gaithersburg Middle School
Gaithersburg, Maryland

Pat (Patricia) Shane, Ph.D.
STEM & ELA Education Consultant
Chapel Hill, North Carolina

Elena Valencia
Coral Mountain Academy
Coachella, California

Janelle Vecchio
Mission Elementary School
Redlands, California

Brittney Wells
Riverside Preparatory Elementary
Oro Grande, California

Kristina Williams
Sequoia Middle School
Newbury Park, California

How Can Medicine Be Delivered More Quickly?

Topic 1 # Properties of Matter

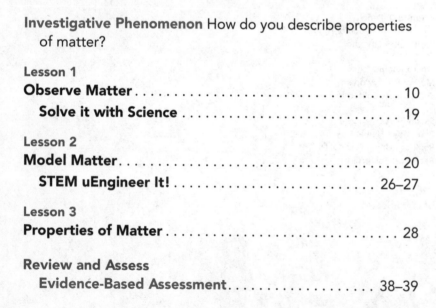

Quest

In this Quest activity, you meet a robotics engineer who presents you with a design challenge. You must design a procedure for a robotic chef to use.

Like a robotics engineer, you complete activities and labs to learn how to identify substances. You use what you learn in the lessons to help design a robot that can identify ingredients.

Find your Quest activities on pages 8–9, 18, 25, 34–35, 36

Career Connection Robotics Engineer page 37

Investigative Phenomenon How do you describe properties of matter?

Topic 2 Changes in Matter

Quest

In this **STEM** Quest activity, you meet a materials scientist who presents you with a design challenge. You must design a model stepping stone for a school habitat.

Like a materials scientist, you complete activities and labs to learn how different combinations of material can make a design more useful. You use what you learn in the lessons to design a model for the stepping stone.

Find your Quest activities on pages 46–47, 55, 62, 74–75, 86–87, 88

Career Connection Materials Scientist page 89

HANDS-ON LAB

uConnect Lab
44

uInvestigate Lab
49, 57, 65, 79

uDemonstrate Lab
92–93

Investigative Phenomenon What evidence do we have that matter changes?

California Spotlight

How Can Medicine Be Delivered More Quickly?

Elevate your thinking!

California Elevate Science takes science to a whole new level and lets you take ownership of your learning. *California Elevate Science* helps you think like a scientist, so you're ready for a world of discoveries.

Exploring California

California spotlights explore California phenomena. Quests are real-life problems that you can solve.

- Start with interesting phenomena
- Spark curiosity with local problems
- Apply knowledge and skills to your solutions

Share Your Ideas

California Elevate Science lets you ask questions, make models and share your ideas.

- Make and use models
- Develop evidence-based arguments
- Practice in speaking and writing

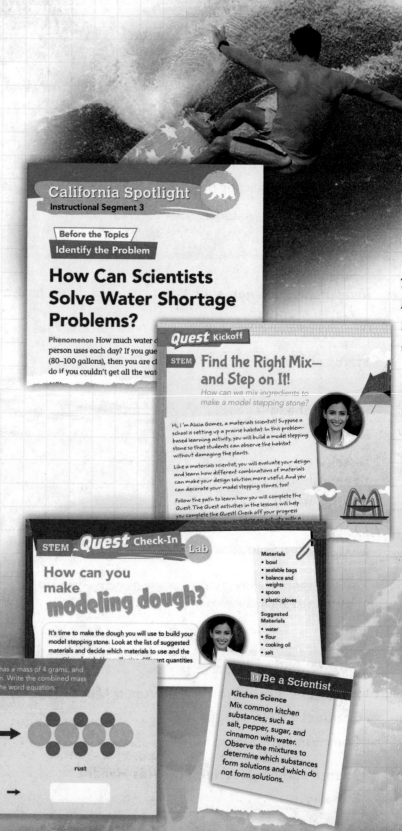

California Spotlight
Instructional Segment 3

Before the Topics
Identify the Problem

How Can Scientists Solve Water Shortage Problems?

Phenomenon How much water d
person uses each day? If you gue
(80–100 gallons), then you are c
do if you couldn't get all the wat

Quest Kickoff

STEM Find the Right Mix—
and Step on It!
How can we mix ingredients to make a model stepping stone?

Hi, I 'm Alicia Gomez, a materials scientist! Suppose a school is setting up a prairie habitat. In this problem-based learning activity, you will build a model stepping stone so that students can observe the habitat without damaging the plants.

Like a materials scientist, you will evaluate your design and learn how different combinations of materials can make your design solution more useful. And you can decorate your model stepping stones, too!

Follow the path to learn how you will complete the Quest. The Quest activities in the lessons will help you complete the Quest! Check off your progress

STEM **Quest** Check-In Lab

How can you make modeling dough?

It's time to make the dough you will use to build your model stepping stone. Look at the list of suggested materials and decide which materials to use and the

Materials
- bowl
- sealable bags
- balance and weights
- spoon
- plastic gloves

Suggested Materials
- water
- flour
- cooking oil
- salt

Model It! In this diagram, each orange particle has a mass of 4 grams, and each red particle has a mass of 1 gram. Write the combined mass of the particles in each space below the word equation.

iron + oxygen → rust

☐ + ☐ → ☐

Be a Scientist

Kitchen Science
Mix common kitchen substances, such as salt, pepper, sugar, and cinnamon with water. Observe the mixtures to determine which substances form solutions and which do not form solutions.

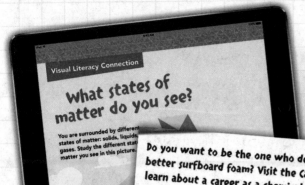

Build Literacy Skills

Connect science to other disciplines like:

- Mathematics
- Reading and Writing
- Visual Literacy

Do you want to be the one who designs an even better surfboard foam? Visit the Career Center to learn about a career as a chemical engineer.

Focus on Reading Skills

Elevate Science creates ongoing reading connections to help you develop the reading skills you need to succeed. Features include:

- Leveled Readers
- Literacy Connection Features
- Reading Checks

Literacy ▸ Toolbox

Use Evidence from Text
Water is formed by the combination of atoms of two different elements—hydrogen and oxygen. Is the smallest particle of water an atom or a molecule? Why do you think so?

Enter the Interactive Classroom

Hands-on experiments, virtual labs, and 3-D expeditions take learning outside the classroom!

- You design cool experiments
- Try online virtual labs
- Go on a Google Expedition

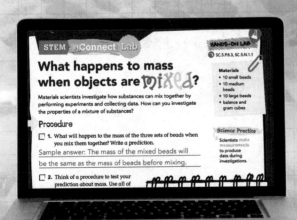

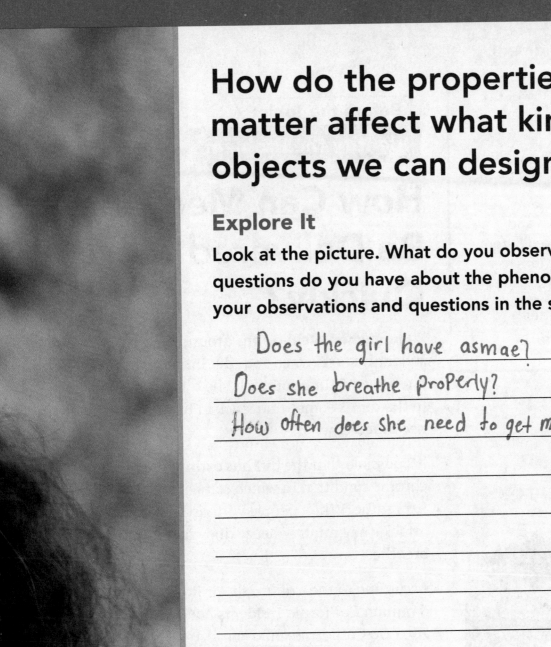

How do the properties of matter affect what kind of objects we can design?

Explore It

Look at the picture. What do you observe? What questions do you have about the phenomenon? Write your observations and questions in the space below.

Does the girl have asmae?

Does she breathe properly?

How often does she need to get medicine?

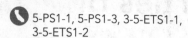

5-PS1-1, 5-PS1-3, 3-5-ETS1-1, 3-5-ETS1-2

Inquiry

- What causes different materials to have different properties?
- How can scientists and engineers use the different properties of matter?

Topics

1 Properties of Matter

2 Changes in Matter

The Airway Clinical Research Center in San Francisco

Before the Topics

Identify the Problem

How Can Medicine Be Delivered More Quickly?

Phenomenon A child runs around on a playground. She suddenly starts wheezing. Her breathing makes a high-pitched whistling sound. Is she allergic to something in the air? Is something stuck in her throat? She might need medicine.

It's possible that the girl has asthma. Asthma is a chronic condition in which some people find it hard to breathe. When people with asthma experience an attack, they might wheeze and cough as they try to breathe.

According to the California Air Resources Board, 5 million California residents have asthma. Close to 700,000 California children currently deal with symptoms of asthma.

The University of California in San Francisco (UCSF) has an Asthma Clinic as part of the UCSF Medical Center. The clinic helps asthma patients manage their condition. UCSF also has an Airway Clinical Research Center. The researchers try to develop better treatment for asthma. They also study allergies.

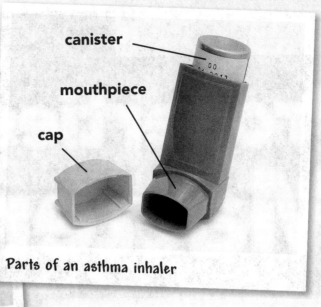

canister

mouthpiece

cap

Parts of an asthma inhaler

This California girl uses her inhaler to control her asthma.

Fortunately, asthma can be controlled. Many patients use devices called inhalers to take medicine for asthma attacks. One common type of inhaler requires the patient to push down on a small canister of pressurized gas while breathing in. The gas propels tiny droplets or particles of medicine from the inhaler. The medicine loosens the muscles around the airways. The airways open up. The patient can breathe more easily.

But inhalers could be improved. Some patients have difficulty breathing in at the same time as they press down. Others may not be able to get the medicine to go past their throat. In these cases, not enough of the medicine goes to the lungs where it is needed. So researchers developed a new kind of inhaler called the breath-actuated inhaler. This inhaler only releases the medicine when the patient breathes in. Other inhalers use different mixtures of liquids and gases, and even solid powders, to deliver medicine more effectively for some patients.

There are sure to be other ways that medicine delivery can be improved. After you study the properties of matter and changes in matter, you will figure out the best way to give medicine to someone having an allergic attack.

Student Discourse With your classmates, discuss why an inhaler is a useful way for many asthma patients to take medicine. How might an inhaler be made easier to use?

Topic 1

Properties of Matter

Investigative Phenomenon
How do you describe properties of matter?

Next Generation Science Standards for California Public Schools

5-PS1-1 Develop a model to describe that matter is made of particles too small to be seen.

5-PS1-3 Make observations and measurements to identify materials based on their properties.

3-5-ETS1-1 Define a simple design problem reflecting a need or a want that includes specified criteria for success and constraints on materials, time, or cost.

3-5-ETS1-3 Plan and carry out fair tests in which variables are controlled and failure points are considered to identify aspects of a model or prototype that can be improved.

See. Think. Wonder.

_____

_____

_____

_____

_____

_____

What's in the b☐x?

You can identify objects by using your senses. What clues help you identify an object?

Procedure

☐ **1.** Each box has a different object inside it. What tests could you use to gather information about the unknown objects?

I would feel the different textures, shapes or smells.

☐ **2.** **SEP Plan an Investigation** Write a plan. Show it to your teacher before you begin. Record your observations.

Observations

I feel the soft, petel-like object. I know it is a flower.

I smell meat. Cubes of soft, bumby meat is stringed on skewers. Kebobs!

Analyze and Interpret Data

3. **SEP Use Evidence** Were you able to identify each object? What evidence did you use?

Yes, I was able to identify each objects. Flowers have delicate, then petals. Kebobs smell delecious!

My Notes and Designs

Draw, Write, Create

I use my five senses to learn about the texture, smells, and tastes of different objects. For example, bricks have a very rough and powdery feeling, while silk is silky smooth. Also, I discovered that pineaple is very rough and watermelon is smooth, while melons are in the middle of both.

Flowers are delicate

marshmallows are soft and gooey. Yum!

Identify the Mystery Material

How can a robot identify materials?

Figure It Out Hi, I'm Maria Alvarez, a robotics engineer. My team is building a robotic chef that can prepare a meal while no one is at home.

In this problem-based learning activity, you will investigate ways that a robot can tell one substance from another. In the Quest, you will evaluate ways to identify substances. You will explore how kitchen ingredients are made of tiny particles. You will also compare substances based on their properties. Finally, you will design a procedure for the robot chef to use!

Follow the path to learn how you will complete the Quest. The Quest activities in the lessons will help you complete the Quest! Check off your progress on the path when you complete an activity with a QUEST CHECK ✓ OFF . Go online for more Quest activities.

🔊 **CA Next Generation Science Standards**

5-PS1-3 Make observations and measurements to identify materials based on their properties.

3-5-ETS1-1 Define a simple design problem reflecting a need or a want that includes specified criteria for success and constraints on materials, time, or cost.

VIDEO

Watch a video about a robotics engineer.

Quest Check-In Lab

Lesson 2

Learn about the particles that make up matter as you explore materials the robot chef will use in recipes.

Quest Check-In Lab

Lesson 3

Use what you learn about the properties of matter to compare materials a robot chef might use in the kitchen.

Quest Check-In Lab

Lesson 1

Learn about the properties of matter and how a robot could tell one substance from another in a kitchen.

Quest Findings

Use your investigations to write a procedure to identify kitchen materials and tell one from another. You will make a chart to guide the robot.

5-PS1-3

CONNECT IT

There are standard units that are used to measure properties, such as weight, length, and time. Using standard units means that someone else—no matter where they live—will be able to know the exact amount you refer to. Why are standard units for weight important when you go shopping for fruits and vegetables?

Wheight is important when you shop becouse you want to know how much exactly you are getting. For example, if your mom sends you to the store for a pound of apples and you grabbed five apples, you grabbed too much. thats why you should wheigh!

uInvestigate Lab

How do we describe materials?

Scientists often use knowledge of different materials to identify what something is. How can you describe an object so that others can identify it?

Materials
- 4 objects

Suggested Materials
- ruler
- balance
- gram cubes

Procedure

☑ 1. Choose three of the objects. Do not let others see them. Write the properties of each object in the Properties column of the table. Use the other materials to help you describe the properties. Do not write the name of the object.

Science Practice

Scientists make observations to produce data.

Object	Properties
RULER	long and thin, with small marks to show measurment.
Scissors	Short, thin, has a handle with two long, thin shiny blades.
TAPE	Sticky on the inside, plain on the outside. Used for sticking things together.

☑ 2. Trade notes with another group. Use that group's descriptions to identify each of the objects.

Analyze and Interpret Data

3. **Evaluate** What information helped you identify each object? What information would have made identifying the objects easier?

Shape and texture, smells and taste; they all help me identifie.

Identify Properties Gather several coins, including at least two that are different kinds. Describe as many properties of each coin as possible. Are the properties of the same kind of coin exactly alike? Why do you think that is so? Which property is most different between the coins that are not the same kind?

Observing Properties

Every kind of material has properties. A property is a characteristic of a material, such as its color and odor. Some materials might have some properties that are the same as the properties of other materials. But no two materials have the exact same set of properties.

You can directly observe many of the properties of a material. When you **observe** something, you use your senses to gather information about it. For example, you use your eyes to observe the color and shape of the materials in the building in the photo. You use your ears to observe that a guitar string makes a specific sound. You observe the hardness and texture of a rock using your sense of touch. In the kitchen, you can observe the properties of foods by tasting or smelling them. When you observe something, you can use the information you gather to describe what you observed. When you **describe** something, you tell about its properties.

Apply Each material in the building has a unique set of properties. Circle the material that has these properties: white, hard, smooth, and in the shape of a rectangle.

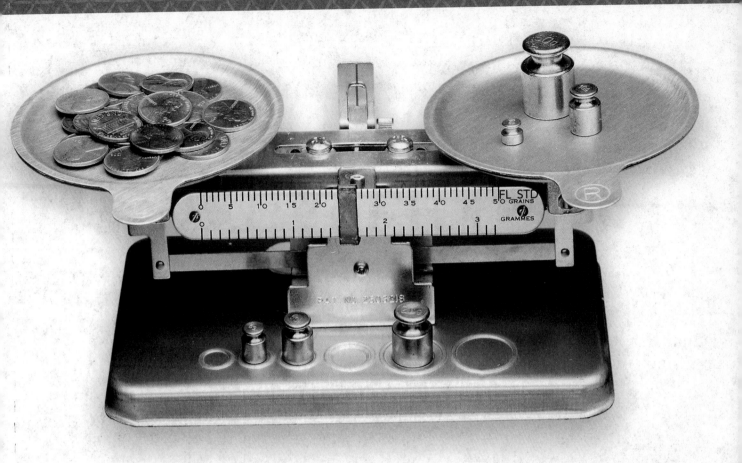

Measuring Properties

You observe some properties by using scientific tools. One way to use tools is to measure. When you **measure** a property, you compare it to a standard unit, or value, for that property. Each unit of measurement is recognized all over the world. For example, you might measure the length of an object using a meterstick. The unit of measurement for length is 1 meter. If the object is 3 meters long, then the measured length of the object is 3 times the length of 1 meter. The meter is the exact same length around the world.

When you measure the weight of an object, you use a balance or a scale. The balance compares the weight of the object to standard weights, such as the gram masses shown in the right pan in the photograph. Each gram mass is marked with a specific amount of grams or kilograms.

Another measurement is how much space a material takes up. This property is measured in liters and milliliters.

Compare Circle the gram mass on the balance pan that you think would measure the largest number of coins.

Can you TELL THEM APART?

Every material has physical properties that you can use to describe it. You can use these properties to tell one material from another. These two blocks have the same length, width, and height. One block is made of wood. The other block is made of steel. How can you tell them apart?

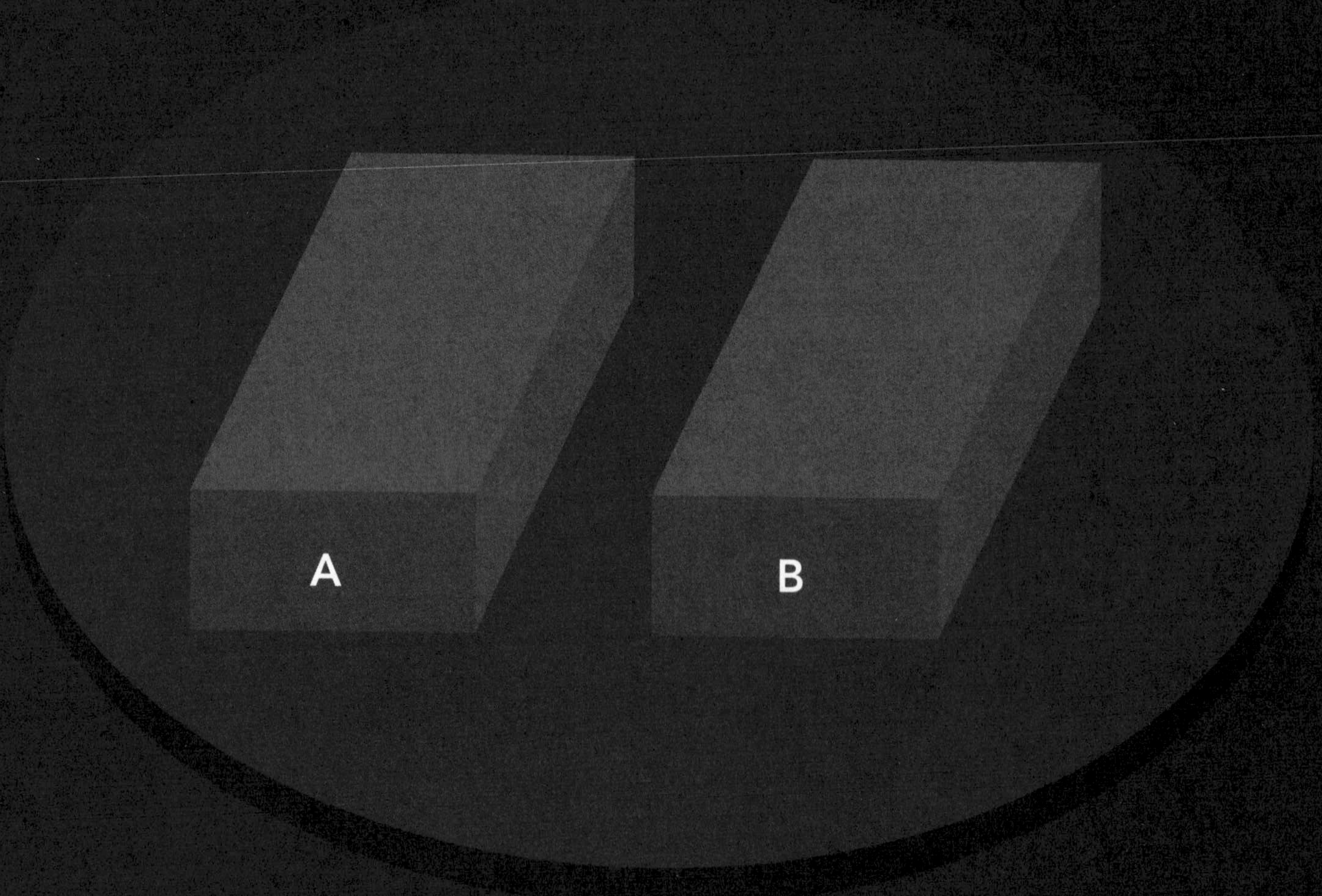

A

B

Which block is heavier?

A **500 g**   B **7,500 g**

How hard are they?

> **!** Which block is made of wood and which block is made of steel? Shade in the block you think is made of steel. Describe how you can identify the material of the blocks.
>
> I know the block is steel, because the nail in the picture wouldn't go in. plus, this block is heavier.

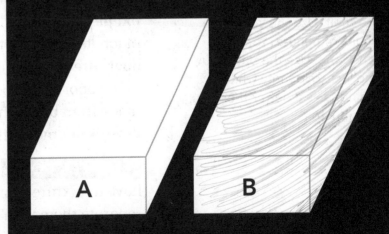

Conductors of Heat and Electricity

You can identify some properties directly by using your senses. Other times, you may need to observe how a material acts with other materials or with energy. If you stir a pot of soup with a metal spoon, the handle of the spoon gets hot. If you stir it with a wooden spoon, the handle does not get hot. A property of the metal is that it is a thermal conductor. A thermal conductor easily moves heat through it. A property of the wood is that it does not easily conduct heat.

Just as some materials transfer heat, some materials conduct electricity. When you connect a light to a battery to make the light glow, you use wires. The wires are probably made of a metal called copper. One property of copper is that it conducts electricity. If you connect the battery and light with string instead of a copper wire, the light does not glow. That is because a property of the string is that it does not easily conduct electricity. How well something conducts heat or electricity is called its conductivity.

Infer Why does the electric cord on a lamp have a layer of plastic around the copper wire?

Becouse it will be safer to use it that way.

Magnetic Materials

Another property of materials is whether they are magnetic, or attracted to a magnet. Many people use magnets to hold notes on a refrigerator. Many refrigerator doors are made from magnetic steel. The magnets sticking to the door are also magnetic. If the refrigerator were made from brass, the magnets would not stick to the door. Brass is not magnetic.

✓ **CHECK POINT** **Use Evidence from Text** If you have a mixture of steel screws and brass screws, you can separate them with a magnet. The magnet will pick up the steel screws but not the brass screws. Circle the text that explains why the screws can be separated this way.

Solubility

If you have ever gone swimming in the ocean, you probably
know that seawater tastes salty. You cannot see the salt in the
water, though, because salt dissolves in water. But if you put a bit
of pepper into a glass of water, the pepper will not dissolve. The
pepper does not appear to change at all. The solubilities of the
two substances are different. **Solubility** is a property of material
that refers to how well it dissolves in another material, such as
water. Salt is soluble in water. Pepper is not. Some substances are
more soluble than pepper but less soluble than salt.

☑ Lesson 1 Check

1. **SEP Analyze Data** Two blocks of shiny, silver metal have the
   same width, length, and height. On a balance, one block weighs
   1.5 kilograms. The other block weighs 2.3 kilograms. How can you
   explain this phenomenon?

   _____

   _____

2. **SEP Explain** What property of a thick cloth pad makes it useful for
   picking up a hot pan on the stove?

   _____

Quest Check-In Lab

How can you observe matter?

A robot chef would need a way to use properties to tell one ingredient from another. How can you learn about the properties of materials by making observations and doing investigations?

Materials
• safety goggles

Suggested Materials
• salt
• sugar
• baking soda
• flour
• white sand
• hand lens
• plastic cups
• water

Procedure

☑ 1. Choose two materials. What are two properties of the materials that you could test?

Baking Soda and salt. Salt is rough and coarse, while Baking Soda is very fine.

☐ 2. Make a plan to test the properties. Show your plan to your teacher before you begin. Record your observations in the table.

 Wear safety goggles.

⚠ Do not taste any of the materials.

Material	Property 1	Property 2
Baking Soda	Very fine	White and Powdery
Salt	rough and coarse	Somtimes Powdered/fine

Science Practice

Scientists make observations to produce data.

Analyze and Evaluate

3. **Compare** How could the robot use the properties to tell one substance from the other?

Each Substance is very different in properties.

Looking for Clues

Detectives on television often use evidence from a crime lab to solve a crime. This also happens in real life. Forensic scientists use clues from a crime scene to figure out what happened and who was responsible. These investigators pay close attention to details. The smallest clue, such as a single human hair, may be the key to solving a crime.

Crime scene technicians might pick up small pieces of dirt and soil that they find at the crime scene. Why would they do that? When you walk outside, bits of soil, sand, and even small pebbles stick to the bottoms of your shoes. Before going inside, you wipe your feet to avoid making a mess. Maybe someone at the crime scene was not so careful. Their tracks might solve the crime. Every kind of soil has particles with different properties—size, shape, and types of materials. By comparing the properties of soil at the scene to the properties of soil on a shoe, forensic scientists can tell where someone walked. That might be just the information that a detective needs.

SEP Obtain Information What information could you obtain by observing a footprint?

I could observe how big, how deep the footprint is.

Model Matter

5-PS1-1

CONNECT IT

This photo, taken from the sky, shows the salt fields at the southern San Francisco Bay area. The salt you use might have come from a similar place. People use tools to break the salt down into smaller pieces. The pieces are crushed further in a factory or by a salt grinder. What do you think would happen to the salt pieces if you kept grinding them?

The salt would grow finer and finer until the salt becomes a fine Powder.

μInvestigate Lab

How can you detect matter without seeing it?

Materials scientists study all kinds of matter. How can you show evidence of matter that you cannot see?

Materials
- safety goggles
- 2 plastic syringes

Suggested Materials
- balloons
- rubber tubing
- cup of water
- plastic straw

Procedure

☑ 1. Pull the plunger to the last mark on the syringe. Observe the syringe. Write a description of what you think is in the syringe.

> I think water is in the syringe. The liquid is clear and runny.

 Wear safety goggles.

☑ 2. Choose materials from the list to test whether matter is in the syringe. Write a procedure to test whether the syringe contains matter. Show your procedure to your teacher before you start.

☑ 3. Record your observations.

Science Practice

Scientists construct arguments based on evidence.

Analyze and Interpret Data

4. **SEP Use Evidence** Explain how your data provided evidence that the syringe contained matter.

> I shaked the syringe. It was full of clear, runny liquid. I know that it is water.

Observations

What is the matter?

All matter, from the very small to the immensely large, is made of smaller particles. How can you observe the magnification of matter?

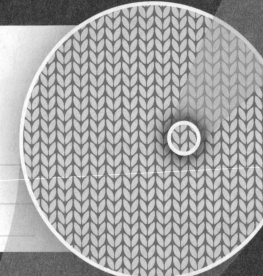

! **Describe** If you were to look closely at a cotton T-shirt, what might you observe with your unaided eye?

The threads and cloth.

Infer Why are you not able to see the loops holding the shirt together with just your eye?

They are too small to be seen with your eyes. You must use a microscope or magnifying glass.

CCC Scale Scientists use magnification to make the fibers look larger. How do the fibers in this image look different from the fibers without magnification?

These fibers are small and make up the loops that hold the shirt together.

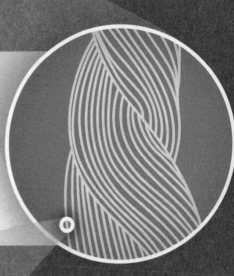

SEP Model Develop a model drawing to show what the particles of the shirt might look like if you could actually see them. Why are you not able to see them?

Disappearance of Particles

Can you make matter disappear? Fill a clear glass with water. Then stir in a spoonful of salt. What do you think happened to the particles of salt? How can you explain your observations?

Divide Matter

When you grind salt, you divide chunks of salt into smaller pieces. These small pieces are still salt. The small grindings have a similar shape to the larger pieces. They taste the same on your food. You can crush them again with a spoon to make salt powder.

Particles

From a distance, a sand castle on a beach looks like a solid object. If you look closely at the castle, you see that it is made of small particles of sand.

All matter is made of particles.

The particles of one kind of matter are different from the particles of other kinds of matter. The particles that make up water are different from the particles that make up sand. The smallest piece of sand that you can see has many more particles than the number of grains of sand in the whole sand castle. You cannot see the smallest particles that make up sand or water with your eyes because they are too small.

☑ Lesson 2 Check

1. Draw Conclusions What is the smallest piece that you could break sand into? Why do you think so?

I don't think you can break the sand grains becouse the are to small to break.

How do you *know* that matter is still there?

When you mix two substances together, the appearance of the matter can change. Are the same particles still there?

Materials
- safety goggles
- 3 plastic cups
- 3 small bowls
- 3 spoons
- salt
- sugar
- baking soda
- water
- wax marker

Procedure

☑ **1.** Label three plastic cups *Sugar*, *Salt*, and *Baking soda*. Pour the same amount of water into each cup.

☑ **2.** Use a spoon to add some sugar into the cup labeled *Sugar*. Stir until the sugar dissolves. Repeat with salt and baking soda. Use different spoons each time. Record your observations.

The water is clear of each cup.

 Wear safety goggles.

⚠ Do not taste.

☐ **3.** How can you find out whether the original materials are still in each cup? Write a procedure. Show your plan to your teacher before you begin. Record your observations.

Science Practice

Scientists use evidence to support their conclusions.

Observations

Analyze and Interpret Data

4. SEP Use Evidence Did your observations present any evidence that matter is made up of small particles? Explain how.

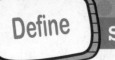
VIDEO

Watch a video about robots in the kitchen.

Robot Pizza

Phenomenon What would you do if you walked into a pizza shop and saw a robot making pizzas in the kitchen? Would you think you were on a movie set? That is just what you would see if you visited the Zume Pizza kitchen in Mountain View, California. The kitchen looks like a manufacturing plant rather than a pizza kitchen. The chefs there have unusual help—from robots! The robots do tasks such as spreading the dough to the right thickness, spreading the right amount of pizza sauce, and removing the pizzas from the oven. The sauce dispenser robot can even adjust the amount of sauce on a pizza according to a customer's preference.

Why does a pizza company use robots rather than people? Robots can make the pizzas faster—more than 370 an hour. That is a lot more than a people-staffed kitchen could make.

Robot Vincenzo places pizza in the oven.

The Zume pizza maker prepares the dough. Robots spread the sauce in seconds.

Define It

Would you like to design a robot chef? Think about the kind of food your robot would make and the tasks it would have to do.

☑ **Student Discourse** The success of a prototype is determined by considering what it needs to do and whether or not it succeeds. Define your design problem. Tell what the criteria for success are for your robot chef.

I think my robot would make donuts. I love the crispy outside, and doughy insids. and the sweet frosting. Yum!

☑ How would you test your robot chef prototype?

I would test him by seeing how fast he can mix dough, frost and fry doughnuts.

☑ Tell two ways your robot chef prototype might fail to make pizza properly.

My robot might add to much sauce, not enough toppings, or make the crust to thick.

☑ What would you do with your prototype if it failed to make pizza properly?

I would try fixing the way it works. If that doesn't work, I would make another, better robot.

☑ **CCC Systems and Models** A robot is a system of parts that work together. Draw your robot on a separate sheet of paper. Label the parts.

5-PS1-3

CONNECT IT

Many places in California have hot air balloon festivals, including the Hot Air Balloon Classic in Sonoma County. Each balloon is made up of three parts: a large balloon with an opening at the bottom, a gas burner under the opening, and a basket where the pilot and passengers ride. To make the balloon rise, the pilot turns on a gas burner to warm the air in the balloon. What are some of the properties of the balloons?

Balloons are big, run on hydrogyn, or hot air, to lift the balloon into the air.

uInvestigate Lab

How can you use properties to identify **solids**?

To identify an unknown substance, materials scientists compare its properties with the properties of known substances. How can you use properties to identify three substances?

Procedure

☐ **1.** You have three substances labeled A, B, and C. Use the table to plan an experiment to identify the three unknown substances. Show your procedure to your teacher before you begin.

☐ **2.** Identify each unknown substance by writing its letter beneath the name of each substance in the table.

Wear safety goggles.

⚠ Do not taste.

Properties of Materials		
Sugar	**Salt**	**Cornstarch**
Sweet solid	*Salty solid*	*no taste*
white solid	white solid	white solid
irregular crystals	cube-shaped crystals	fine powder
dissolves in water	dissolves in water	does not dissolve in water
solution is not very conductive	solution is very conductive	does not form solution

Science Practice

Scientists interpret data when they analyze results of an investigation.

Analyze and Interpret Data

3. SEP Use Evidence What evidence did you use to identify each unknown?

I tasted the different substances, and felt the different textures.

Food Coloring in Water

With an adult, fill one bowl with hot water and one bowl with cold water. Put one drop of food coloring in each bowl. What differences do you observe? How can you explain your observations?

States of Matter

Scientists organize all matter according to its state. When you **organize** something, you sort it. Matter can be organized into three main states—solid, liquid, and gas. Water is a solid when it is ice. It is a liquid when you drink it. The gas form of water is called water vapor. The state of a material is due to the motion of its particles. A material can change from one state to another as the motions of its particles change. Water is a solid when it is very cold and its particles vibrate in place. It turns into a liquid when it is heated and its particles move about. Water becomes a gas when it is very hot and its particles move very fast.

Solid

Liquid

Gas

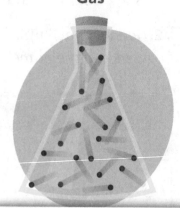

The particles of a solid do not slide easily past each other. They vibrate, or move back and forth, in place.

The particles of a liquid can move past each other.

The particles of a gas move very fast and spread out evenly to fill available space.

Model It!

Suppose that you are a particle. With your classmates, act out how particles behave in a solid, liquid, and gas. How did you show each state of matter?

If I was a particle in a solid, I would not move, just vibrate back an forth. If I was a liquid, I would be able to move around. If I was a gas, I would be very speedy.

Temperature

The **temperature** of an object is a measure of how fast its particles are moving. The higher the temperature, the faster the particles move. Different scales are used for measuring temperature. In science, you probably will find the temperature at which a substance melts given in degrees Celsius (°C). In a recipe, cooking temperature is most likely given in degrees Fahrenheit (°F). Both units are accurate measures of temperature.

Collect Data This food thermometer shows the temperature of the meat. What is the temperature? Be sure to identify whether the temperature is given in Fahrenheit or Celsius.

The temperature of the meat is at 160 °F.

Mass and Volume

The amount of matter in a substance is its **mass**. Scientists usually measure mass in units of grams (g) or kilograms (kg). To find the mass of an object, you can compare it to other objects that have a known mass. On a balance, the sides will be uneven, like those in the photo, when the masses are different.

The amount of space an object takes up is its **volume**. Volume can be measured in milliliters (mL). Solid and liquid materials have a definite volume. They take up a certain amount of space. Gases also have volume. The volume of a gas will change to fill all of the space available.

Student Discourse Describe the relationship between mass and volume.

Crosscutting Concepts ▸ Toolbox

Stability and Change
One main goal of science is understanding how things change. Think about the properties discussed on these pages. How easily do you think these properties can change? Rank them from most changeable to least changeable.

Color

The physical properties of a material can be observed, measured, and described without changing the material. Color is a physical property of matter. Color is an easy property for identification because you can determine the color of something just by looking at it. You can often organize various types of matter based on similarities and differences in color.

Apply Give an example when using color to identify a substance would be important.

For Example, if you lose track of different juices, you will need to see the color of the juice to sort it. For Example, celery juice will be green, and orange juice will be orange.

Texture, Hardness, and Reflectivity

When you touch a solid object, you can feel whether it is smooth, lumpy, grooved, spongy, or rough. This surface structure that you can feel by touching a material is its texture. Hardness is another property of a solid that you can feel. If something is hard, it tends to keep its shape when you push it or strike it. If it is soft, it tends to bend.

You see objects because they reflect, or give off, light. Reflectivity is a measure of how bright an object appears when light hits it. The more light they reflect, the brighter objects appear.

brick

☑ CHECK POINT **Use Evidence from Text**
If you could touch the brick and copper, how would you describe the texture? Which has greater reflectivity?

Brick is very rough, or coarse.
Copper is very soft, although it tends
to bend when it is heated. Copper has
more reflectivity.

copper

☑ Lesson 3 Check

1. **Claim** When a small brick and a large fluffy cushion are put on two sides of a balance scale, the scale is level. Which object has more matter?

   The large fluffy cushion has more matter.

2. **Evidence** Cite evidence from the text to support your claim.

   The cushion is larger and is stuffed with cotton,
   with means the cushion has more matter.

3. **Reasoning** How does the evidence support your claim?

How can you compare the properties of matter?

Before you can program the robot, you must understand the properties of the materials the robot will be sensing. How can you learn about the properties of familiar materials?

Suggested Materials

- cups
- water
- hand lens
- wooden block
- metal coin
- sugar
- salt
- flour
- baking soda
- white sand
- paper
- spoon

Procedure

☐ 1. Choose four objects from the list of materials. Record which objects you have chosen in the first column of the table.

☐ 2. Choose three different physical properties of the objects that you will test. Choose from these properties: color, texture, solubility, reflectivity. Record the properties that you will test in the top row of the table.

☐ 3. **SEP Plan an Investigation** Plan how you will test the properties. Write your plan and have your teacher approve it.

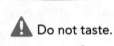

⚠ Do not taste.

Science Practice

Scientists use evidence to support explanations.

☐ 4. **SEP Conduct an Investigation** Test the three properties. Record your data and observations in the table.

Properties of Materials

Material	Property 1 _____	Property 2 _____	Property 3 _____
1			
2			
3			
4			

Analyze and Interpret Data

5. **Evaluate** Suppose you had an unknown sample and knew that it was one of the four materials you tested. How could you identify which material you had based on the properties you tested?

_____

_____

_____

_____

6. **Evaluate** What is another property that you could use to tell which of the four substances you have? Explain your answer.

_____

_____

_____

👆 **INTERACTIVITY**

Organize data to support your Quest Findings.

STEM ▸ Identify the Mystery Material

How can a robot identify materials?

You have learned about the properties of matter. Now you will develop a test that a robot chef could use to be certain that it is using the right ingredients in a recipe.

Design a Procedure

Several common ingredients in the kitchen are white solids. These include flour, salt, sugar, and baking soda. Write a procedure to test an unknown material and identify it as one of these white solids.

SEP Construct Explanations

Will your tests allow the robot to identify the material if it is one of the four ingredients listed above? How do you know?

_____

_____

_____

_____

_____

Procedures

I know that salt can be very coarse, or rough.

_____

_____

_____

_____

_____

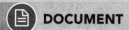
Career Connection

Robotics Engineer

Robotics engineers design and build new robots, program them to perform specific tasks, and find new things for robots to do. Many robots perform tasks in factories. Robotics engineers design these robots so they can handle tools. They also write computer programs that instruct the moving parts what to do.

You might see a simple robot that vacuums the floor. Cars that carry passengers with no driver have been tested on roads. Robots help doctors in hospitals, run equipment on farms, and play with children. All of these robots were designed and built by robotics engineers.

Robotics engineers use math and science in their daily work. These engineers must be creative to find new ways to use robots to do tasks. Robots have traveled to the deep ocean, gone into burning buildings, and even explored volcanoes. Engineers figure out the best way to design a robot for each task.

Reflect How do engineers use creative thinking as they design a robot?

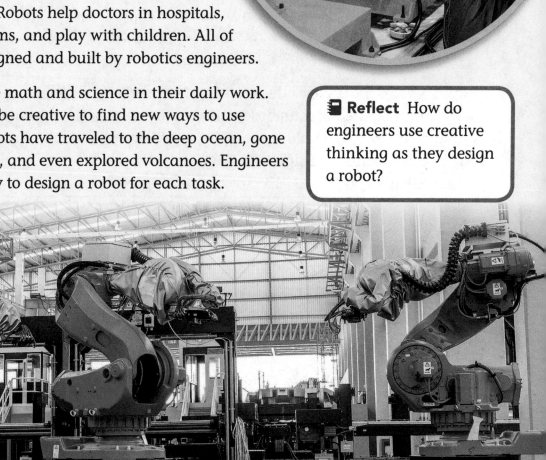

Read this scenario and answer questions 1–5.

A scientist in a manufacturing lab was given a substance to identify. The substance was known to be one of four possible substances. The chart shows some properties of the four. Equipment for the investigation included beakers, water, vinegar, and a hand lens.

Properties of Substances				
Property	**calcium carbonate**	**calcium sulfate**	**sodium bicarbonate**	**fructose**
Solubility in water	not soluble	not soluble	soluble	soluble
Color	white	white	white	white
Particle appearance	powder	crystals	powder	crystals
Makes bubbles in vinegar	yes	no	yes	no

1. **Evaluate** The chart shows the scientist's tests and results. Someone in the lab suggested that an observation of the color of the substance would be important. Explain why color would or would not be a useful observation in this investigation.

   Somtimes different substances could change color
   after they are soaked in liquid.

2. **Evaluate** The scientist observed one unknown substance using a hand lens. It was made up of crystals. What conclusions could be made based on this observation? Check all that apply.

   ☐ The substance is calcium carbonate.

   ☑ The substance might be fructose.

   ☑ The substance is not sodium bicarbonate.

   ☐ The substance can only be calcium sulfate.

   ☐ The substance is neither fructose nor calcium carbonate.

3. **Collect Data** If the scientist thinks the substance is either sodium bicarbonate or calcium carbonate, what test could be used to decide which it is?

   A. Dissolve the substance in water.

   B. Observe the color of the substance.

   C. Put the substance in vinegar.

   D. Weigh the substance.

4. **SEP Plan an Investigation** The scientist considered starting with tests that could identify the substance in one step. Could any of the tests make an identification in one test? If so, identify which substance or substances could be identified by that test.

   For Sodiom Bicarbanate, and calcium carbonate, he could try dissolving it in water. Calcium Carbonate is not soluble. But Sodium Bicarbanate is soluble.

5. **Evaluate** The scientist recorded these observations.

Property	Observation
Solubility in water	soluble
Color	white
Particle appearance	powder
Makes bubbles in vinegar	yes

What was the unknown substance?

   A. calcium carbonate

   B. calcium sulfate

   C. sodium bicarbonate

   D. fructose

uDemonstrate Lab

How do you know what it is?

Phenomenon When scientists test substances, they make observations. Then they compare the substance to a substance with known properties. How can you identify unknown materials by comparing test results to known properties?

Procedure

☐ **1.** What tests will you perform to identify the unknown substances? You should use at least two different tests.

_____

_____

_____

_____

_____

☐ **2. SEP Plan an Investigation** Write a procedure for the tests of the unknown substances. Use all of the listed materials. Show your procedure to your teacher before you begin.

_____

_____

_____

_____

_____

_____

Materials
- safety goggles
- 2 plastic cups
- 2 unknown substances
- hand lens
- water
- magnet
- spoon
- conductivity tester

 Do not taste any of the materials.

 Wear safety goggles.

Science Practice

Scientists make observations to answer questions.

3. Record your data.

Substance	Appearance	Magnetic	Soluble	Conductive in Water
salt	white crystals	no	yes	yes
sugar	white crystals	no	yes	no
iron fillings	dark pieces	yes	no	no
activated carbon	dark pieces	no	no	no
unknown #1				
unknown #2				

Analyze and Interpret Data

4. Evaluate What were the properties of the substances that you used for identifying the unknown substances?

_____

_____

_____

5. CCC Structure and Function Was your test able to show differences among all of the four known materials? Provide evidence to support your answer.

_____

_____

_____

6. Draw Conclusions Were you able to identify the two unknown substances? Explain.

_____

_____

Changes in Matter

Investigative Phenomenon

What evidence do we have that matter changes?

Next Generation Science Standards for California Public Schools

5-PS1-1 Develop a model to describe that matter is made of particles too small to be seen.

5-PS1-2 Measure and graph quantities to provide evidence that regardless of the type of change that occurs when heating, cooling, or mixing substances, the total weight of matter is conserved.

5-PS1-4 Conduct an investigation to determine whether the mixing of two or more substances result in new substances.

3-5-ETS1-1 Define a simple design problem reflecting a need or a want that includes specified criteria for success and constraints on materials, time, or cost.

3-5-ETS1-2 Generate and compare multiple possible solutions to a problem based on how well each is likely to meet the criteria and constraints of the problem.

See. Think. Wonder.

_____

_____

_____

_____

_____

_____

What happens to mass when objects are mixed?

Materials scientists investigate how substances can mix together by performing experiments and collecting data. How can you investigate the properties of a mixture of substances?

Materials
- 10 small beads
- 10 medium beads
- 10 large beads
- balance and gram cubes

Procedure

☐ 1. **Student Discourse** What will happen to the mass of the three sets of beads when you mix them together? Discuss your answer with a partner.

_____

_____

Science Practice

Scientists make measurements to produce data during investigations.

☐ 2. Think of a procedure to test your prediction about mass. Use all of the listed materials. Share your procedure with your teacher before you begin.

☐ 3. Make a bar graph to show your data. Label each bar on the x-axis. Label the units on the y-axis.

Analyze and Interpret Data

4. **SEP Use Evidence** What happens to the mass of objects when they are mixed?

_____

_____

_____

_____

Observations

Bead	Small	Medium	Large	Mixture
Mass (g)				

Mass (g)

Bead size

My Notes and Designs

Jasmina

Draw, Write, Create

Mass: The mass of somthing is how much matter it contains.

small   medium Large

Mix

The mass is larger and heavier, but the beads are not blended; just mixed.

When different sized beads are mixed together, the beads don't completely mix together. Instead, they will get mixed up, but it will be easy to sort becouse of the size of different beads.

When things are mixed, the more larger the mass is. Mass is the amount of matter in an object.

Quest PBL

Find the Right Mix— and Step on It!

How can we mix ingredients to make a model stepping stone?

Figure It Out Hi, I'm Alicia Gomez, a materials scientist! Suppose a school is setting up a prairie habitat. In this problem-based learning activity, you will build a model stepping stone for the habitat so that students can observe the habitat without damaging the plants.

Like a materials scientist, you will evaluate your design and learn how different combinations of materials can make your design solution more useful. And you can decorate your model stepping stones, too!

Follow the path to learn how you will complete the Quest. The Quest activities in the lessons will help you complete the Quest! Check off your progress on the path when you complete an activity with a QUEST CHECK ✓ OFF. Go online for more Quest activities.

Quest Check-In

Lesson 1

Learn about the states of matter and their properties to help you develop a list of criteria and constraints to guide the development of your model stepping stone.

🧭 **CA Next Generation Science Standards**

5-PS1-4 Conduct an investigation to determine whether the mixing of two or more substances result in new substances.

3-5-ETS1-1 Define a simple design problem reflecting a need or a want that includes specified criteria for success and constraints on materials, time, or cost.

3-5-ETS1-2 Generate and compare multiple possible solutions to a problem based on how well each is likely to meet the criteria and constraints of the problem.

Quest Check-In Lab

Lesson 4

Use what you learn about mixtures and solutions as you revise your "concrete" formula to get the best product. Then build your model stepping stone.

Quest Check-In Lab

Lesson 3

Find out about chemical changes and how they affect the model "concrete" you will make.

Quest Findings

Use your model to think about other important features of a concrete stepping stone. Suggest how you would change your model. Retest your model.

Quest Check-In

Lesson 2

Apply what you learn about physical changes in matter as you sketch a model for your stepping stone.

States of Matter

5-PS1-1, 5-PS1-2, 5-PS1-4

CONNECT IT

How many different types of matter do you see in this picture of explorers at the South Pole?

_____

_____

_____

_____

_____

uInvestigate Lab

Is goop **solid** or *liquid*?

Most of the materials around you are clearly solid, liquid, or gas. Could there be substances that are hard to classify?

Procedure

☐ 1. In the bowl, add one cup of cornstarch to 100 mL of water. Mix the substances with your hands or with the wooden spoon. If the mixture stirs easily, add a bit more cornstarch. If some of the cornstarch stays powdery, add a bit more water. You can also add a drop or two of food coloring.

☐ 2. When the cornstarch and water are thoroughly mixed, stir it slowly with the spoon. Then stir it very quickly. Record your observations.

☐ 3. Pick up some of the mixture in your hand. Try to roll it into a ball. Keep pushing on the mixture while rolling it. Then stop pushing on the mixture while you hold it over the bowl. Record your observations.

☐ 4. What are some other investigations that you can do with the mixture?

_____

_____

_____

Analyze and Interpret Data

5. Classify Can you classify the mixture as a liquid or a solid? Explain your answer.

_____

_____

_____

Materials

- water
- cornstarch
- spoon
- bowl
- safety goggles
- measuring cup
- graduated cylinder, 50mL

Suggested Materials

- food coloring

 Wear safety goggles.

 Do not taste.

Science Practice

Scientists use evidence to make explanations.

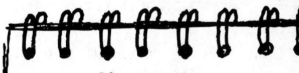

Observations

What states of matter do you see?

You are surrounded by different states of matter: solids, liquids, and gases. Study the different states of matter you see in this picture.

Solids are always around you.

! Identify two solids you see. Describe how you can identify that these objects are solids.

Gases are always there but usually not visible. **Gas** is a form of matter that does not have a definite shape or definite volume.

❗ Identify two objects that you see interacting with gases.

Windmills and rain interact with gases.

Liquids are often nearby.

❗ Identify three liquids you see. Describe how you can identify them as liquids.

Water and Juice, or dew are liquids you can see.

Solids

Solid, liquid, and gas are the three states of matter. Most substances can exist in any of these states, depending on temperature. A **solid** can be identified because it has a definite shape. When you place a solid object such as an ice cube in a cup, it does not spread to cover the bottom of the cup. An ice cube is solid and keeps its shape in the cup. As the ice cube warms, it may melt. Then it is no longer a solid.

1. **Claim** Can ice have different shapes and still be the same kind of matter? _Yes._

2. **Evidence** Cite evidence from the text to support your claim.

   Ice can be a solid when it is frozen, and a liquid when it melts.

3. **Reasoning** Explain how the evidence supports your claim.

   _____

   _____

Liquids

When an ice cube melts, it forms water, which is a liquid. A **liquid** is a substance that has a definite volume but does not have a definite shape. If you pour liquid from a shallow, round bowl into a tall glass, its shape changes a lot. The new shape matches that of the inside of the glass, while the volume of the liquid in the bowl and in the glass are the same.

Liquids flow from one place to another unless something holds them in place. For example, the water in the Gabilan Mountain waterfall rushes downward because nothing is stopping it.

Reflect What did you learn in this lesson that helped you understand something you observed in the past but could not explain? Write your thoughts in your science notebook.

Gabilan Mountains, central California

Gas

Matter surrounds you all of the time. The air that you breathe is matter in the form of gas. If you move your hand back and forth quickly, you can feel the matter even though you cannot see it.

Gas is a form of matter that does not have a definite shape or a definite volume. You can **differentiate**, or tell the difference between, a gas, a liquid, and a solid because gases in a container always fill the entire volume of the container. Although some gases have color that you can see, most common gases are colorless. You can detect them by their effects on other objects. If you blow through a straw into a glass of water, you will see bubbles of gas coming up through the water. Moving air causes a wind turbine to turn.

Student Discourse With a partner, discuss the characteristic that differentiates a gas from a liquid or a solid.

You cannot see a gas although you can feel it. But you can see and feel a solid and liquid.

Science Practice
▶ Toolbox

Designing Solutions
Engineers design solutions to problems by applying scientific knowledge. Suppose you must move a toy boat across a pond. How can you use your knowledge of gases to move the boat?

☑ Lesson 1 Check

1. **CCC Systems and Models** An ice cube is placed in a jar and left on a table. The ice cube melts. A lid is placed on tightly. The jar sits on a sunny window sill, and all of the liquid water becomes a gas. Differentiate the three states of matter in this system model.

Water will evaporate, or turn into gas, when it is heated. An Ice cube will melt when warmed.

2. **CCC Structure and Function** Mercury is a metal that is sometimes used in thermometers because it flows easily and takes the shape of the thermometer tube. Explain why mercury can be used in a thermometer but other metals cannot.

It's a Matter of Materials

Some types of matter may be useful for making a stepping stone. Other types of matter will not work as well. Answer the questions below to help decide some of the properties that materials for your stepping stone will need.

1. **SEP Define a Problem** For your stepping stone project, describe the things that the stone must be able to do. List some of the criteria that will help you figure out what kind of design would work.

_____

_____

_____

2. **CCC Cause and Effect** Identify the state of matter that is most likely to meet your criteria. Will all materials in the state of matter that you identified meet the criteria for your design problem? Explain your answer.

_____

_____

_____

_____

3. **CCC Structure and Function** What other characteristics are important in the materials you will use?

_____

_____

_____

Physical Changes

5-PS1-1, 5-PS1-2

CONNECT IT

This building is knocked down using heavy equipment. The materials, such as concrete and steel, become smaller pieces. Tell why you think the materials do or don't change.

I think the concrete and steel will not change. The size may change, but the peices will still be concrete and steel. The mass may become larger or smaller, but the smaller peices of concrete and steel are still concrete and steel.

Which properties are affected by temperature?

When materials scientists develop new materials, they must consider how temperature affects the properties of a material. Which properties are affected by temperature?

Materials
- aluminum foil
- piece of thin rubber
- sugar cubes
- safety goggles
- water
- plastic cups
- spoon
- large dish of ice water
- large dish of warm water

Procedure

☐ **1. SEP Plan an Investigation** Use all the materials. Think of a way to test how temperature affects solubility and flexibility, and how shiny a material appears. In the table, identify which substance you will use to test each property.

☐ **2.** Write a procedure to test each property. Show your plan to your teacher before you start. Record your observations.

Wear safety goggles.

Do not taste.

Observations

	Sugar	Aluminum foil	Rubber
Property tested			
Observations			

Science Practice

Scientists *collect data* to answer questions.

Analyze and Interpret Data

3. CCC Energy and Matter Which physical changes were affected by the temperature difference and which were not affected by the temperature difference?

_____

_____

_____

_____

Changes in Shape

Matter often changes size and shape. A **physical change** is a change in some properties of matter that does not form a different kind of matter. A melted juice pop, torn paper, and broken glass are all examples of physical changes.

Some physical changes give matter a different shape. If you drop a cell phone, the glass screen might shatter. The glass has undergone a physical change. Some of its properties have changed, but the properties that make it glass are still there. It is still hard and clear. It still does not react with most substances. Cutting paper and stretching a rubber band are also physical changes. After breaking glass or stretching a rubber band, you still end up with glass or rubber. The mass of the parts of the broken phone screen is exactly the same as the mass of the unbroken screen.

SEP Explain What pattern can you observe to indicate that a physical change does not make a new substance?

If you tear up a paper, it will still be paper and the mass will be the same. It is a physical change.

Changes in Temperature

The temperature of an object or material is one of its physical properties. A change in temperature is a physical change. A cold object feels different from how the same object feels when it is warm. When the temperature of an object changes, other physical properties might change at the same time. You can establish this concept with a balloon. When you **establish** something, you make the truth clear. If you put an inflated balloon in the freezer, it will shrink. That is because the volume of air will change when the air temperature changes. After you take the balloon out of the freezer, it will become warmer. It will then return to its original size.

Metal can also change its size and shape when its temperature changes. The railroad tracks in the photograph appear to be warped and bent. That change in shape happened when the tracks became hot. The metal expanded. That caused the tracks to bend. In very hot climates, people must inspect the tracks often to keep them safe.

CCC Cause and Effect Metal railroad tracks shrink when they get colder. Why do you think shrinking does not cause the tracks to warp?

When it grows warmer, the metal on a track becomes soft, causing it to bend.

As the balloon and the air particles in it get cooler, the balloon pushes the air particles closer together. As a result, the particles take up less space and the balloon gets smaller.

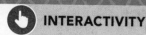
Science Practice
▶Toolbox

Construct Explanations
Water freezes at 0°C/32°F. At a warmer temperature, water will be a liquid. How can you use this information to predict the precipitation that will fall on a given day?

Changes in State

Another physical change of a substance is a change of its physical state. As liquids get colder, their particles slow down. When the temperature gets cold enough, the particles can only vibrate in place. They cannot slide past each other, so the liquid becomes a solid. This change is called freezing. The opposite change can occur when a solid is heated. As its particles gain energy, they again move past one another. The solid melts to form a liquid.

When a liquid turns into a solid, the temperature at which this happens is called the freezing point. That temperature is called the melting point when a solid turns into a liquid. Each substance has its own melting point. The melting point can be used to help identify a material.

The melting point of water is 0°C. Below that temperature, water is solid ice. Above the melting point, water is a liquid.

Apply Concepts Label the liquid and solid in the photos. Predict the temperature for each state.

_____

_____

_____

Evaporation takes place when particles leave a liquid and become a gas. Particles evaporate from a liquid when they are at the surface of the liquid and are moving upward with enough speed. This is how rain puddles and wet clothes become dry.

If the temperature of a liquid is high enough, particles will change to a gas not only at the surface but also throughout the liquid. As gas particles move quickly upward through a liquid, bubbles of gas form under the surface of the liquid. The boiling point of a liquid is the temperature at which this occurs. As with the melting point, each substance has its own boiling point. The boiling point can be used to help identify a substance. The boiling point of water is 100°C.

☑ **CHECK POINT** **Use Evidence from Text** How can you use the melting point or boiling point to help identify a substance?

_____

_____

_____

_____

∪Be a Scientist

Saltwater Ice Cubes
With an adult, fill an ice cube tray with water. In half of the spaces, use salt water. Use fresh water in the others. Make sure to keep track of which are which. Put the ice cube tray in a freezer. Check your tray one hour later. What can you infer from your observations about the properties of water and salt water?

☑ Lesson 2 Check

1. CCC Scale, Proportion, and Quantity How does the mass of water formed by melting an ice cube compare to the mass of the ice cube?

_____

_____

2. Explain How can you tell that a change in a material is a physical change?

_____

_____

Quest Check-In

Stepping Stone Properties

For your stepping stone, you might want to use a material that does not change easily. Draw a model of what your stepping stone will look like. Apply what you have learned about physical changes as you sketch your model stone. Consider the size, shape, and physical state of the stone. Label some of the physical properties of the stepping stone.

Design

I like a strong, flat rock.

They don't change very quigly and they are strong and beutiful.

QUEST CHECK ✓ OFF

Look Out for Flying Rocks!

Phenomenon The UCLA Collection of Meteorites in Los Angeles, California, contains more than 300 meteorites collected from hot deserts. Eighty of these meteorites are from California. Meteorites are small chunks of rock and metal that have traveled through space and fallen to Earth. More than 50,000 meteorites have been found on Earth. Perhaps one is waiting for you to discover it!

Canyon Diablo meteorite from the UCLA Collection of Meteorites

You can use the physical properties to figure out whether a rock is a meteorite. Almost all identified meteorites are made mostly of iron and nickel, so many times a magnet will stick to them. If the rock is round like a smooth pebble, it is not a meteorite. Most often, as the meteorite falls through space, different parts of it melt or evaporate. This causes most meteorites to be unevenly shaped. They may even look like they have been burned. Meteorites are also much heavier than other rocks that are the same size. If your rock passes all these tests, it might be a meteorite. However, the only way to be sure is to have a lab test its true properties.

Connect What makes this meteorite different from Earth's rocks?

Meteorites are heavier and are made of iron or nickel, so they are magnetic.

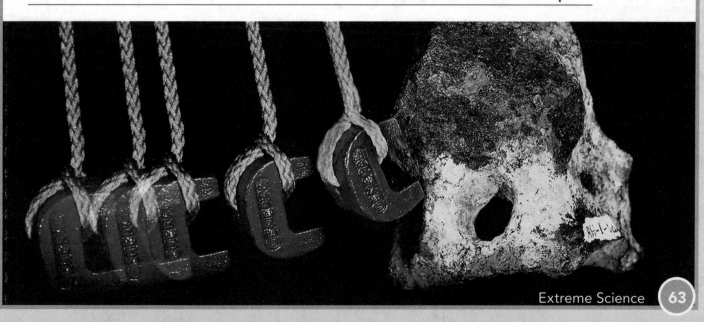

Chemical Changes

5-PS1-2, 5-PS1-4

CONNECT IT

Manufacturing engineers can change materials such as scraps and grass clippings into charcoal. They place the matter into a large metal container and heat it. How do you know the charcoal is not the same material as the grass clippings?

Grass clippings will not burn into charcoal becouse green grass cannot burn. Dry grass will burn and turn into Charcoal.

New Substances

If you take a piece of charcoal and break it into pieces, the smaller pieces will still be charcoal. However, something different happens when you burn charcoal. Burning is an example of a chemical change. A **chemical change** is a change that produces one or more new substances. When charcoal burns, a chemical change occurs in which charcoal and oxygen form new substances. These new substances are ashes and gases that you cannot see.

How can you identify chemical changes?

Materials scientists conduct investigations to provide evidence that their product does what it is supposed to do. What evidence can you look for to show that a chemical change has occurred when substances are mixed?

Procedure

☐ 1. Write a hypothesis about chemical change when substances are mixed.

_____

_____

☐ 2. **SEP Plan, Conduct, and Investigate** Choose at least one liquid and one dry material. Write a procedure to test your hypothesis about chemical change. Remember to think about your variables. Show your procedure to your teacher before you start.

☐ 3. Record your observations.

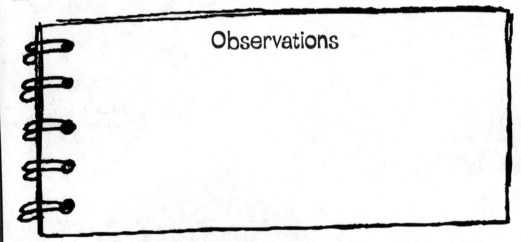

Observations

Analyze and Interpret Data

4. **Use Evidence** How does your data support your hypothesis?

_____

_____

Materials
- safety goggles
- plastic cups
- spoons
- graduated cylinder, 50 mL

Suggested Materials

Dry materials
- sugar
- baking soda
- salt

Wet materials
- vinegar
- water
- lemon juice

 Wear safety goggles.

 Do not taste.

Science Practice

Scientists collect data when they investigate a scientific question.

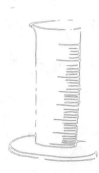

Changes in Substances

Let's look at the changes that take place in another familiar example—baking a cake.

1 Each ingredient used to make a cake has its own properties.

2 You mix the ingredients together, but they keep their own properties.

3 The mixed ingredients are put in the heated oven.

4 A new substance forms. The baked cake has different properties.

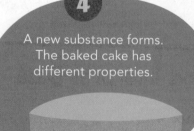

How do you know they are chemical changes and not physical changes?

The texture, taste and color is different.

Explain
List two other chemical changes you see in your life.

When you fry eggs, the new substanse will still be eggs, but the texture will be different.

Particles and Chemical Changes

When a chemical change occurs, the particles that make up the original substances rearrange to form new substances. It is not always easy to tell whether a substance has changed chemically. Evidence of chemical change may include the release of heat or light, a change in color, a new smell, gas bubbles, or the formation of a solid.

You can use building blocks to model a chemical change. In the picture, the blocks represent particles of matter. They are connected to form two substances. You can connect them in other ways to form different substances.

Model It! The blocks are combined to show two different substances. Draw how you could rearrange the blocks to make two other substances. Use all six blocks.

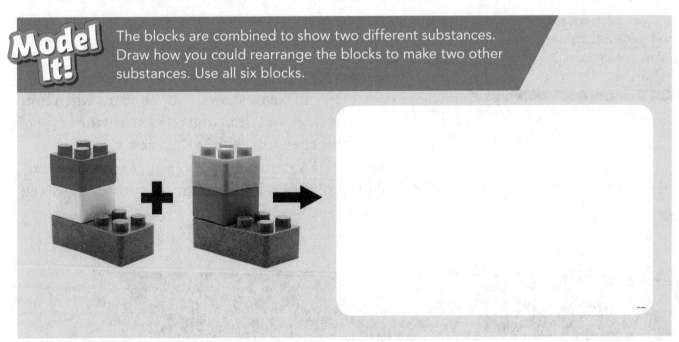

Like the building blocks, the particles that make up matter rearrange during a chemical change. In the example below, the balls each represent a different kind of particle in the two substances. After a chemical change happens, the same particles are in the two new substances, but they are arranged differently.

original substances   new substances

Conservation of Matter

Scientists have done many experiments to test whether mass changes during chemical changes or physical changes. Their data **support**, or back up, the idea that mass stays the same before and after any change—no matter what. From this evidence, scientists developed the law of **conservation of matter**. The law states that in any chemical change or physical change, the total mass of the matter does not change.

In a chemical change, all the particles that make up the original substances end up in the new substances. So, the combined mass of the substances before a chemical change is the same as the combined mass of the substances after the chemical change.

The particle diagram below shows what happens when iron combines with oxygen gas. Iron and oxygen are the original substances in this chemical change. The new substance that forms is rust. You can use the diagram to compare the combined mass of the original substances to the mass of the new substance.

Model It! In this diagram, each orange particle has a mass of 4 units, and each red particle has a mass of 1 unit. Write the combined mass of the particles in each space below the word equation.

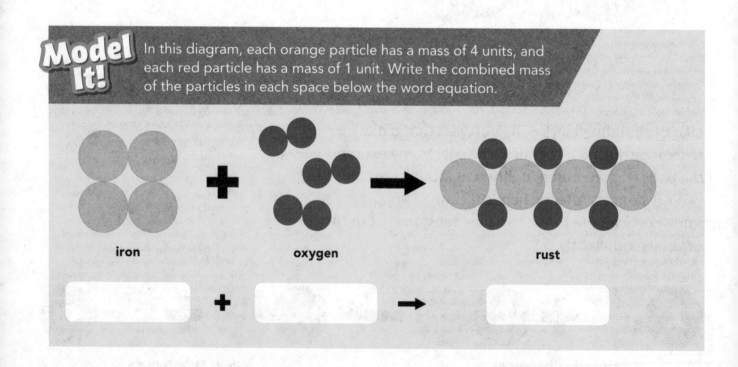

iron + oxygen → rust

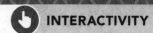
Look at the nails. The shiny new nails are made of iron. Over time, the nails can rust. Rusting is a chemical change. The change occurs when the iron on the surface of a nail combines with oxygen gas to form rust.

When you observe one or more substances change into one or more new substances, you observe a **chemical reaction**. The nails rust as a result of a chemical reaction. The iron in the nails and oxygen gas react to form rust.

☑ CHECK POINT **Use Evidence from Text** If you measure the mass of nails before and after they rust, will the masses be the same? Explain your reasoning.

_____

_____

_____

_____

_____

_____

Is matter conserved?

Read the information for each step to see what happens during the chemical reaction. Write a math equation to model how the masses of the original substances and the new substances compare.

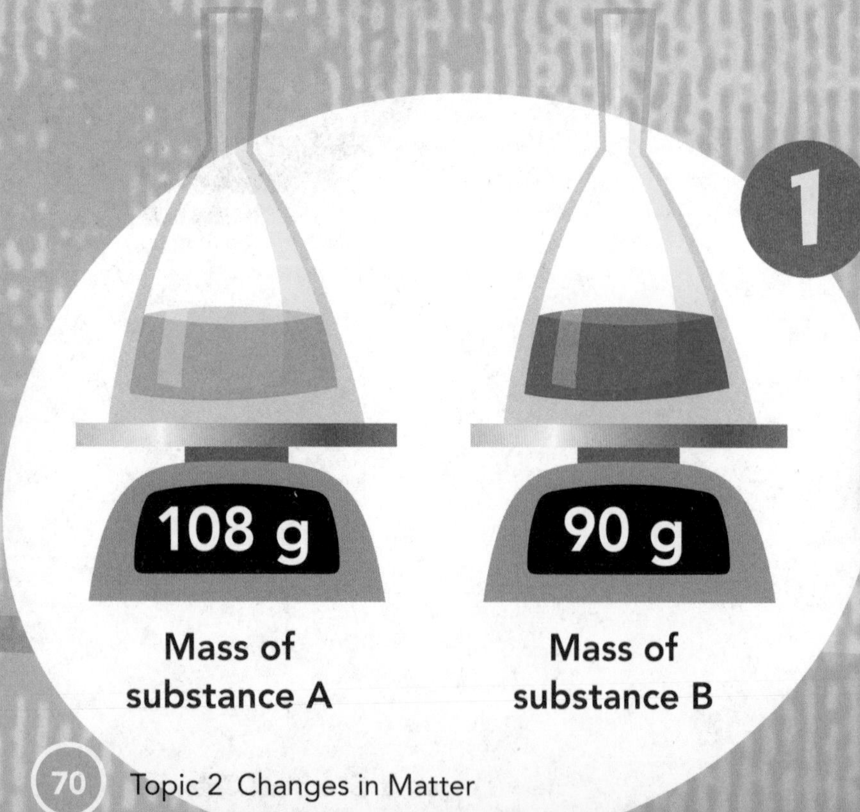

1

Each flask holds a different substance. Read the mass on each scale. The mass seen on each scale is the mass of the substance. The mass of the flask has been subtracted.

108 g

Mass of substance A

90 g

Mass of substance B

Two new substances

The color of the liquid substance is different from the colors of substances A and B. A new solid substance is visible, too. These observations provide evidence of a chemical change.

3

Write the total mass of the two new substances. (Ignore the mass of the beaker.) Hint: Use the information in step 1.

_____

2

Substances A and B mixing

When substances A and B are poured together, they mix. Assume that no gases are released or added to the liquid.

Identify a Chemical Change

Conduct an investigation to determine whether the mixing of two substances results in new substances. First, use a spoonful of sand and a glass of water. Record the properties of the sand and of the water. Then, mix the two materials. Record your observations. Next, repeat the procedure but use one-fourth of a cup of milk and two spoonsful of vinegar. Did a chemical change happen when the sand and water were mixed? Did a chemical change happen when the milk and vinegar were mixed? How do you know?

Examples of Chemical Changes

Chemical changes happen in the kitchen all the time. A chemical change occurs when a chef makes fresh cheese. To make fresh cheese, the chef adds lemon juice to whole milk. Once the two liquid ingredients are mixed, solid pieces start to form. The solid pieces, called curds, are chunks of the fresh cheese. They form as a result of a chemical change. To prepare the cheese to eat, the chef separates the curd from the liquid.

Different kinds of cheeses are produced by further processing the curds. For example, to make soft, stringy cheese like mozzarella, the curds are kneaded. Many cheeses are "aged." During aging—which can take months—bacteria in the cheese chemically change the cheese. Gouda is an example of an aged cheese.

📔 **Write About It** Do a close read of the paragraph above. Identify the main idea. In your science notebook, explain how the author uses key details to help support the main idea.

You may have noticed another chemical change. Over time, some pennies change color from copper to green. This color change happens because of a chemical change. The copper metal that makes up a penny combines with oxygen gas to form a green substance. The green substance is copper oxide.

Identify What two substances is copper oxide made of?

_____ **+** _____ ➡ **copper oxide**

Student Discourse How do you know a chemical change has occurred? Explain your reasoning to a partner.

_____

_____

_____

_____

☑ Lesson 3 Check

Kolab recorded the properties of two liquid substances, A and B. He then mixed them together in a closed beaker, and the liquid changed colors. He recorded the properties of the mixed substances.

Substance	Color	Odor	Mass
A	colorless	none	3.6 grams
B	colorless	foul	2.1 grams
A + B	yellow	none	?

1. ☑ **CHECK POINT** **Use Evidence from Text** Is this a chemical change? How do you know?

_____

_____

2. **SEP Analyze Data** Write the mass of the mixture of substances A and B. How can this mass be used as evidence of the conservation of matter?

_____

_____

How can you make modeling dough?

Materials
- bowl
- sealable bags
- balance and weights
- spoon
- plastic gloves

Suggested Materials
- water
- flour
- cooking oil
- salt
- sand
- glitter
- food coloring

It's time to make the dough you will use to build your model stepping stone. Look at the list of suggested materials and decide which materials to use and the quantities of each. How will using different quantities of materials affect the dough?

 Do not taste.

 Wear plastic gloves.

Design Your Model

☐ **1. SEP Develop a Model** Make a list of criteria your stepping stone needs to meet.

_____

_____

_____

Engineering Practice

Engineers develop models to test that a design meets specific criteria.

My Formula

_____

_____

_____

_____

_____

_____

_____

☐ **2.** Choose your materials and list them on the formula card.

☐ **3. SEP Design Solutions** Make two different formulas by changing the quantities of materials.

☐ **4.** Measure each material and record the amount on the card.

☐ **5.** Share your formula card with your teacher before you start.

☐ **6.** Make your different formulas.

☐ **7. SEP Interpret Data** Conduct an investigation to produce data to serve as the basis of evidence about which formula works best. Use fair tests in which variables are controlled. Consider how many trials you should do for each formula.

Evaluate Your Model

8. Use Evidence Do your results show whether a chemical change occurred? Provide evidence to support your answer.

_____

_____

_____

9. CCC Cause and Effect Which formula met your criteria for a model stepping stone? Provide evidence to support your answer.

_____

_____

_____

10. SEP Use Models How does your modeling dough compare to concrete that is used to make stepping stones?

_____

_____

_____

uEngineer It! Define STEM

INTERACTIVITY

Go online to evaluate and compare competing designs.

Foam Sweet Foam

Phenomenon Surfing is a popular sport along the coast of California. Most surfboards are made of foam. Basic surfboards are often made of polyurethane foam, which floats easily in the water because it is very light. It is also strong. Other boards are often made of polystyrene foams. These foams are lighter than polyurethane foam, but they are not as strong. Besides, some polystyrene foams can sometimes absorb water. That, of course, is not a good quality for a product designed to float!

Recently, a group of chemists and engineers designed a new type of foam for surfboards. This new foam is not only lighter than any other surfboard foam. It also lasts longer and floats better.

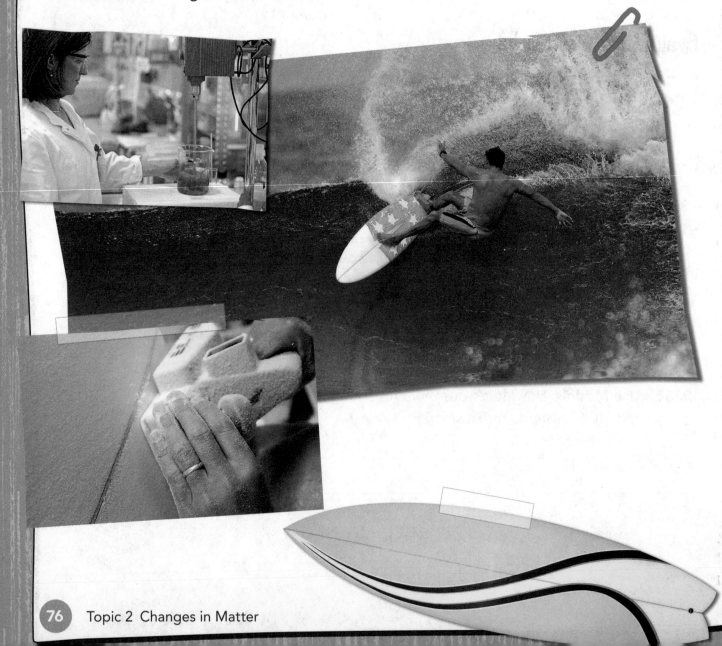

Define It

Foams are made using a series of chemical and physical changes. They are used in the design of many products, including automobiles, helmets, pillows, and food containers. There are many types of foam besides the kinds used in surfboards, and they each have different properties. Engineers improve existing technologies to increase a product's benefits. Suppose you work for a company that builds playground equipment. The company wants to build a new piece of equipment for small children.

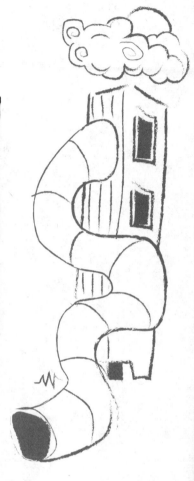

- ☐ Choose one piece of equipment that can be built using foam or that you think should include foam.

- ☐ **Define the Problem** Define the purpose of the foam in the product you choose.

- ☐ Brainstorm some **criteria** and **constraints** that could help you judge which foam is best for your product.

It should...	It should not...

- ☐ **Student Discourse** Discuss how you will test your design.

- ☐ Draw your piece of equipment.

Mixtures and Solutions

5-PS1-1, 5-PS1-2, 5-PS1-4

CONNECT IT

When you mix two or more different colors of paint, you make a new color. Tell whether you could separate the new color back into the old colors. Why or why not?

_____

_____

_____

_____

_____

_____

_____

_____

How can you separate a mixture?

Knowing physical properties of matter can help scientists separate individual substances from a material. How can you use physical properties to separate the parts of the mystery mixture?

Materials

- mixture
- plastic cups
- water
- sieve
- magnet inside a plastic sealable bag
- safety goggles
- spoon

 Wear safety goggles.

 Do not taste.

Procedure

☐ **1.** Observe the mixture. What parts of the mixture can you identify?

_____

_____

_____

☐ **2. SEP Plan an Investigation** Plan a way to separate the components from one another. Use all of the materials. Show your procedure to your teacher before you start.

☐ **3. SEP Conduct an Investigation** Separate the components of the mixture and record your observations.

Science Practice

Scientists *conduct investigations* to provide evidence.

Analyze and Interpret Data

4. Use Tools How did the magnet help you separate the components of the mixture?

_____

_____

_____

_____

_____

_____

Observations

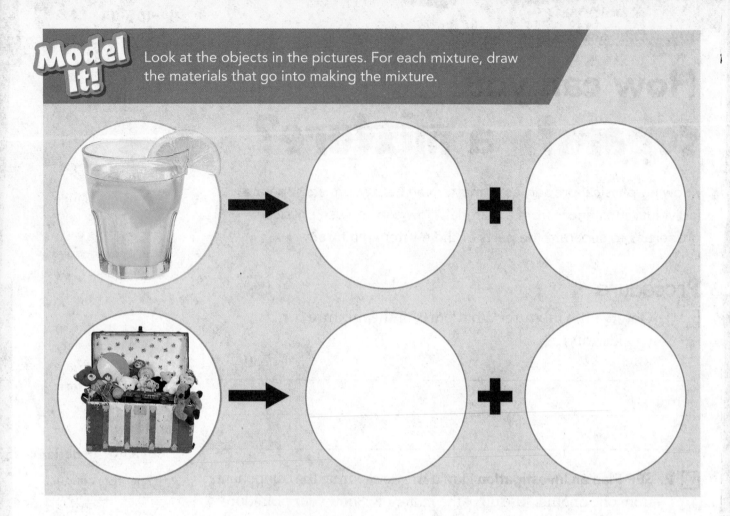

Mixtures

If you mix peanuts and raisins, each of the substances keeps its own properties. In a **mixture**, different materials are placed together, but each material in the mixture keeps its own properties. In the nut and raisin mixture, you can easily separate the nuts from the raisins. Different parts of a mixture can be separated from the rest of the mixture. When sand and blocks are mixed, you could separate the blocks from the mixture by picking them out. You could also use a strainer to separate the parts.

Some mixtures cannot be separated as easily as the nuts and raisins. For example, iron ore is a rock that is a mixture of different substances. One of these substances is iron. Large factories separate the iron from the other **components**, or parts, of the mixture. To do this, they use a lot of energy to make the iron liquid and separate it from the other components.

Solutions

If you place salt in water, the salt and water form a mixture. But the salt seems to disappear. That is because the salt water is a solution. A **solution** is a mixture in which substances are spread out evenly and do not settle to the bottom of the container. The substance that is dissolved in a solution is called the solute. The substance in which the solute is being dissolved is called the solvent. When the salt dissolves in the water, individual salt particles separate from the solid and spread evenly throughout the water. Ocean water is a familiar example of a salt and water solution. The water has a salty taste because salt is dissolved in the water. You can make solids dissolve in a liquid faster by stirring or heating the solution. Grinding a solid into smaller pieces will also help it dissolve faster.

Not all solutions are made by dissolving a solid in a liquid. Two liquids can make a solution. For example, vegetable oils used in cooking might be a solution of soybean oil and sunflower oil. A gas can also dissolve in a liquid. For example, water can contain multiple dissolved gases.

✓ **CHECK POINT** **Cite Evidence from Text** Circle the words or phrases on this page that support the explanation of how to change the speed of the dissolving process.

Math ▸ Toolbox

Graph Data A student mixes 5 grams of sand, 8 grams of salt, and 20 grams of water. What will be the mass of the mixed substances? Make a graph to show your data.

when is a mixture also a solution?

Some mixtures have parts that can be easily separated.

Draw the parts that make up the mixture.

In a solution, the parts mix evenly and cannot be easily separated.

Draw the parts that make up the solution.

Separating Solutions

The components of a solution keep their own properties, but they usually cannot be separated as easily as other mixtures. That is because the components of a solution are evenly mixed. You cannot pick out chunks of one material from the mixture. You cannot remove a solid component with a filter paper. Its particles are spread out and become part of the liquid. However, the parts of a solution can be separated. To separate the parts of the solution, you use physical properties of the substances in the solution.

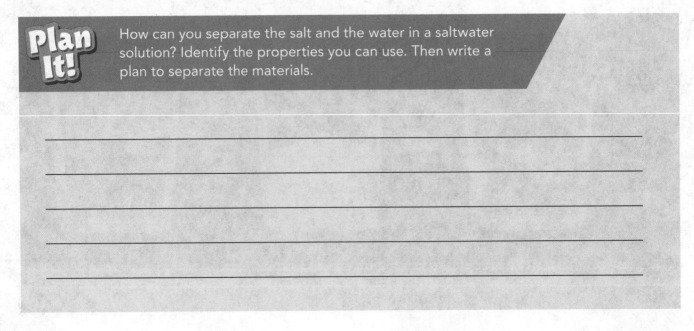

Plan It! How can you separate the salt and the water in a saltwater solution? Identify the properties you can use. Then write a plan to separate the materials.

_____

_____

_____

_____

_____

Student Discourse Suppose a solution contains 0.2 g of solute in 50 mL of solvent. The solution is separated into two equal parts. Discuss with a partner how you can figure out the amount of solute and solvent in each of the two parts. Find evidence in the text to support your answer. Then calculate the amounts.

Mixtures and Solutions

Remember that all solutions are mixtures, but not all mixtures are solutions. You can tell the difference by observing the mixture closely. A solution is the same in all parts. For example, clear apple juice is a solution. Any samples of the juice are just alike, and there are no separate particles in the mixture. Fresh squeezed orange juice is not a solution. You can see chunks of orange in the mixture. If you let the orange juice pass through a filter paper into a glass, it will separate. The glass will contain a clear liquid, and the filter paper will have solid orange pulp. You cannot separate a solution by filtering it. To separate a solution, you have to cause a physical change to one or more of its components.

Infer If you separate orange juice by filtering it, is the liquid in the glass a solution? Why or why not?

_____

_____

Make Meaning Mixtures and solutions are important to people in their everyday lives. In your science notebook, identify mixtures or solutions that you use every day. Why are they important to you?

☑ Lesson 4 Check

1. **☑ CHECK POINT** **Use Evidence from Text** Sugar consists of fine white crystals. Salt also consists of fine white crystals. A mixture of salt and sugar consists of fine white crystals. If they are mixed well, do the sugar and salt form a solution? How do you know?

_____

_____

2. **SEP Construct an Argument** Can a solution consist of more than two components? Explain your answer with evidence.

_____

_____

How can you make a new and improved formula?

Materials
- bowl
- sealable bags
- balance and weights
- spoon
- plastic gloves

Suggested Materials
- water
- flour
- cooking oil
- salt
- sand
- glitter
- food coloring
- pebbles
- copper wire

Consider how well your stepping stone model met the criteria and constraints of your engineering problem. How will using different materials or quantities of materials affect the model?

Design Your Model

☐ **1.** Write any criteria that your model did not address well.

_____

_____

☐ **2.** Choose your materials and list them on the formula card.

 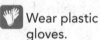 Do not taste.

Wear plastic gloves.

My New Formula

_____

_____

_____

_____

_____

_____

Engineering Practice

Engineers **redesign a solution** after testing to find a solution that meets specific criteria.

3. Write a new formula by changing the materials or quantities that you use in the model. Measure each material and record the amount on the card.

4. Share your formula card with your teacher before you start.

5. Make your new formula.

Evaluate Your Model

6. Test Decide how to test your new model in order to determine whether it meets the criteria and constraints better. Write down your test.

_____

_____

_____

_____

7. Evaluate Did the new formula improve the model? Provide evidence to support your answer.

_____

_____

_____

_____

8. SEP Use Models How does your new model compare to concrete that is used to make stepping stones?

_____

_____

_____

_____

_____

_____

STEM Find the Right Mix— and Step on It!

How can we mix ingredients to make a model stepping stone?

When you made the dough, you provided criteria. With a group, discuss if your model stepping stone met the criteria you set.

Discuss how you would change your model to improve it. Write a procedure for testing your improved model. Retest your model.

Construct Explanations

Did the change to your model improve it? How do you know?

_____

_____

_____

Procedure to Retest

_____

_____

_____

_____

_____

_____

Do you think the same change to the concrete stepping stone would result in a better product? Why or why not?

_____

_____

_____

Career Connection

Materials Scientist

Materials scientists developed many of the materials we use daily. They develop new materials and improve existing ones. Many problems faced by society today are a result of not having the right materials. Materials scientists might make a material that is thinner, lighter, or stronger than the ones currently in use.

Many of the materials that materials scientists develop are used for medical purposes. For example, they might develop a new material for heart valves or as part of a hip replacement. Other materials are used in dental applications and surgeries. Some are used to deliver drugs. The products made by materials scientists touch every part of our lives.

📑 **Reflect** In your science notebook, write about what you would like to study if you were a materials scientist.

Read this scenario and answer questions 1–5.

A young scientist found 2 liters of an unlabeled solution of white liquid in a glass jar. She wanted to find out what some of the properties of the substance were. So, she tested the substance. Her results are in the table.

Mystery Substance Property	Observation
Color	white
Odor	slightly sweet
Boiling point	100.5°C
Reaction with acid	solution separated into clear liquid and white solid matter, sour smell produced.

1. **SEP Use Math** The scientist added 0.5 grams of a solid to 2 grams of the liquid in a closed container. Can you predict the total weight of the substances after the materials were mixed? Explain your answer and give the weight if possible.

_____

_____

_____

_____

2. **CCC Cause and Effect** Which conclusion can you draw about the effect that happened when the solution was mixed with an acid?

   A. The solution was separated by a physical change only.

   B. The solution was broken down into its smallest particles.

   C. The solution was changed chemically into new substances.

   D. The solution was changed physically.

3. Collect Data What evidence supports your answer to question 2?

  A. Liquid is left behind when matter is broken down.

  B. New substances with new properties were observed.

  C. The sour odor produced is evidence of waste products.

  D. Part of the liquid solution changed state to become solid.

4. CCC Cause and Effect The scientist noticed evidence of a gas rising from the solution while boiling it. Afterwards, she noticed that there was less mass remaining in the solution than when she started. Which of the follow statements about this phenomenon are true? Select all that apply.

  ☐ Boiling resulted in a change in the state of matter of the solution.

  ☐ The solution changed from a gas to a liquid.

  ☐ The solution changed from a liquid to a gas.

  ☐ Boiling did not result in a chemical change in the solution that altered the solution's properties.

  ☐ Boiling destroyed some of the matter in the solution.

5. Evaluate Which of the following is evidence of a chemical change having taken place?

  A. New substances appeared when substances were mixed together.

  B. The solution became solid as the temperature was lowered to −5°C.

  C. The volume of the solution increased when the solution was heated.

  D. Gas could be observed escaping from the solution when it was heated.

How does mass change when you make glop?

Phenomenon When materials scientists mix ingredients, they produce data that shows what happens to mass. They make observations about any changes that occur when ingredients are mixed. What do you think will happen when you mix glue, water, and borax solution?

Procedure

1. Make glop using 30 mL of glue, 15 mL of colored water, and 15 mL of borax solution. What will happen to the mass of the ingredients after they become glop? Write a hypothesis.

_____

_____

_____

_____

 Wear safety goggles.

 Do not taste.

 Wash your hands when finished.

2. Write a procedure to test your hypothesis about mass. Use all of the listed materials. Show your procedure to your teacher before you begin.

_____

_____

_____

_____

_____

_____

Science Practice

Scientists make measurements to produce data during investigations.

☐ **3.** Make a table to show your data. Your table should display evidence that relates to your hypothesis.

Analyze and Interpret Data

4. Calculate Add together the masses of the glue, water, and borax solution. How does this combined mass compare to the mass of the glop?

_____

_____

_____

_____

_____

Observations

Substance	Mass of substance and cup (g)	Mass of substance (g)
Glue		
Colored water		
Borax solution		
Glop		

5. Use Evidence Did a chemical reaction occur? Provide evidence to support your answer.

_____

_____

_____

_____

6. Draw Conclusions Is your hypothesis supported by your data? Explain.

_____

_____

_____

_____

Conduct an Investigation

Now that you have studied the topics in this segment, you can complete the activity.

Solids, Liquids, Gases

Some asthma patients also use long-term control medicines. These medicines are often taken as pills or injections. Pills are usually taken every day. Injections are usually given once or twice a month. These medicines work to hold off symptoms, but an inhaler is still used if symptoms flare up suddenly.

Medicine can be delivered to the body's system in many ways. Different delivery methods work best for different types of medicines. A medicine can be a solid, a liquid, or a gas.

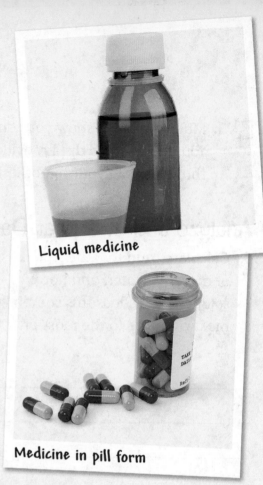

Liquid medicine

Medicine in pill form

Describe How might a patient take a solid medicine? How might a patient take a medicine that is liquid? What about a gas?

_____

_____

_____

_____

Study the table to find information about common delivery methods.

Infer Circle the method that you think would get the medicine into a patient's body as fast as possible. What kind of matter is it? Explain why it would be the fastest.

_____

_____

_____

_____

Describe What changes in matter occur as a pill travels through the body?

_____

_____

_____

_____

_____

_____

_____

Delivery Method	State of Matter	Where Medicine Goes	Features
Pill (tablets, capsules)	Solid	Blood stream via swallowing	May be difficult for some patients to swallow May have more side effects Is convenient to transport
Oral liquid	Liquid	Blood stream via swallowing	Is easy to swallow May have more side effects May need to be kept cold Patient must measure correct amount
Injection	Liquid	Injection sites: Into the muscle for quick delivery to the bloodstream; between skin and muscle for long-acting	Must be injected by someone who knows how Can cause slight pain May need to be kept cold
Inhaler	Liquid mixed into a gas, or a solid powder	Lungs, with some amount ingested	May be difficult for some patients to use

A Better Medicine Delivery System

Have you ever been stung by a bee or other insect? Most people experience some pain and swelling where they were stung. Some people, however, are allergic to bee stings. They may have difficulty breathing after being stung. This is similar to the symptoms of an asthma attack.

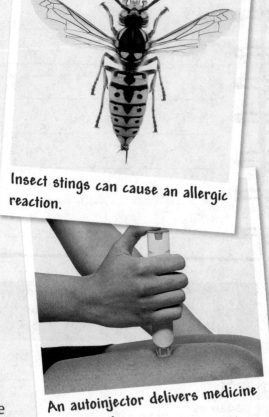

Insect stings can cause an allergic reaction.

When a person has a severe allergic reaction and can't breathe, they need medicine immediately. Otherwise, they might faint from not breathing. One way to ensure that a person has medicine when it is needed is to carry a device called an autoinjector. The person can then inject a liquid medicine into his or her body. The medicine will help the person start to breathe again.

The autoinjector is about the size of a large highlighter. The medicine inside it should not be exposed to extreme hot or cold temperatures, either below 15° C (59° F) or above 30 °C (86° F). It should also not be exposed to light or air.

An autoinjector delivers medicine immediately.

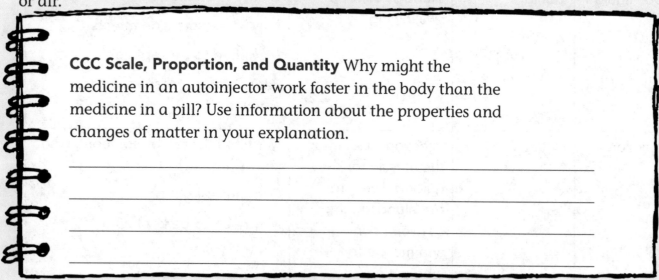

CCC Scale, Proportion, and Quantity Why might the medicine in an autoinjector work faster in the body than the medicine in a pill? Use information about the properties and changes of matter in your explanation.

_____

_____

_____

_____

Use what you have learned about medicine delivery to propose the best way to treat a severe allergic reaction.

Define the Problem What is the problem you are trying to solve?

_____

_____

_____

Criteria What does your solution need to do to be successful?

_____

_____

_____

_____

_____

Constraints What are some limits on your solution?

_____

_____

_____

Generate Solutions Write at least two different solutions to the problem.

_____

_____

_____

_____

_____

Communicate Collaboratively Write an advertisement for one of your solutions and present it to the class. Compare how well the solutions meet the criteria and constraints of the problem, and choose the one you think is best.

Science Practices

Ask Questions

Science is the study of the natural world using scientific tools and methods. The natural world includes things such as matter, energy, the planets, and living things. It does not include things such as opinions about art or music.

A scientist asks questions and then tries to answer them. For example, a scientist might wonder how a large whale finds its food deep in the ocean. The scientist could first study what others have already learned. Then the scientist could investigate questions that have not been answered. Questions could include "How can a whale hold its breath underwater when it makes a deep dive?" Or, "How does a whale find food in the darkness of the deep ocean?"

Ask Questions What question would you ask about the animal in the photograph?

_____

_____

_____

_____

_____

_____

_____

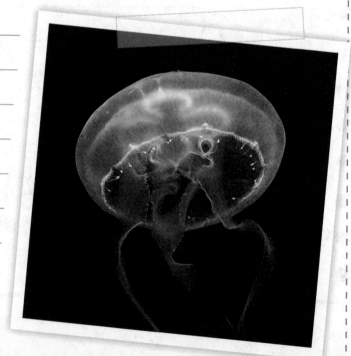

SEP.1 Asking questions and defining problems
SEP.3 Planning and carrying out investigations
SEP.4 Analyzing and interpreting data

Carry Out Investigations

Scientists use investigations and experiments to do their work. Part of an investigation is to observe the natural world to learn about how it works. When scientists make observations, they do not change anything. Scientists collect data from their observations. Quantitative data are expressed as numbers. Qualitative data describe something, such as how it smells or what color it is.

Scientists also investigate the world using experiments. In an experiment, scientists make a change to the object or process they are observing. For example, the amount of salt dissolved in ocean water is not the same everywhere. To find out how quickly salt dissolves in water at different temperatures, a scientist might put identical amounts of salt and water in several containers at different temperatures. The scientist changes the temperature of the containers and measures the time the salt takes to dissolve in each. The part of the experiment that the scientist changes is called the independent variable. The part that changes as a result is called the dependent variable. In this case, the independent variable is temperature, and the dependent variable is the time the salt takes to dissolve. All scientific investigations include collecting data.

Plan an Investigation A scientist is investigating how the amount of salt in water affects the growth of young fish. What are some quantitative data that the scientist can record?

_____

_____

_____

Science Practices

Science Tools

Scientists use tools to take measurements when they collect data. They also use tools to help make observations about the natural world. Scientific tools expand the type of observations that can be made.

Tools for measuring include rulers to measure length, certain glassware to measure volume, thermometers to measure temperature, and balances to measure mass. Different types of tools are needed for taking very small or very large measurements. It is important to use the right tool for the measurement that is to be taken.

Tools that expand what we can detect and measure include microscopes and telescopes. These tools allow people to observe things that are too small or too far away to see.

Cause and Effect Red tides occur when the population of tiny algae grows. The organisms can make toxic substances that harm wildlife and make the water unsafe for people. How would scientists use a microscope when they study a red tide?

_____

_____

_____

Digital Tools

Many modern tools operate using microprocessors or computers. These objects are digital tools. Digital tools include measuring tools such as digital balances and thermometers. They also include tools that scientists use to record and analyze data. Many scientific instruments have a computer that guides data collection and records results. Digital cameras are often a key part of telescopes, microscopes, and other tools used to make observations.

A solar panel provides power for the digital instruments and computer on this buoy. The instruments can measure changes in the ocean.

Computers and other digital devices make data collection faster. Processors can respond to changes and record data much faster than a human observer can. Computers are also important for keeping records and analyzing large numbers of data. Computers and other digital devices are an important part of communication networks that allow scientists to share data and results.

Communicate Scientists communicate in different ways. How could a scientist use a computer to communicate with another scientist?

_____

_____

_____

Science Practices

Analyzing and Interpreting Data

Scientists use empirical evidence when they study nature. Empirical evidence is information that can be observed and measured. Scientific conclusions are always based on evidence that can be tested. These observations and measurements are data that can be used to explain the natural world.

Measurements and observations provide scientists with evidence of changes. For example, when a natural system changes, the change can affect organisms in the system. Scientists can observe and record the changes, such as how many organisms are living in an area at one time compared to another time. Then the scientists can analyze those data to make predictions about the effects of other changes.

Scientists analyze measurements and observations to answer scientific questions. Analyzing measurements of changes in an ecosystem can provide information about how different parts of the natural system work together.

Measure The temperature of water affects ocean currents and marine habitats. How could scientists get empirical evidence about the temperature of the water? Why is this empirical evidence?

_____

_____

_____

_____

_____

Using Math

Careful measurements are necessary for collecting reliable data. Scientists make measurements several times to be sure that the results can be repeated. In general, scientists use digital instruments to collect quantitative data.

Scientists use mathematics to analyze quantitative data. They record measurements and compare them to find out what changes and what stays the same. A number of measurements can be compared to show if something changes over time. Mathematical analysis can also show how fast a change occurs.

When a scientist makes a claim based on evidence, other scientists can check the claim. When other scientists check the claim and find similar results, the claim or findings are supported by similar evidence.

Evaluate How do numerical data from measurements make it easier to compare results in an investigation?

_____

_____

Research ships carry many instruments that gather data.

Science Practices

Constructing Explanations

After scientists analyze data, they use their results to construct explanations of natural phenomena. A scientific explanation often uses the change in variables to relate one change to another. For example, as conditions in marine ecosystems change, organisms living in the water might change in response. Scientists observe changes in ecosystems and study populations of organisms to learn about effects of changes. Then they construct explanations about the organisms.

Developing and Using Models

Scientists often use models to help them understand something. Models are objects or ideas that represent other things. A model only shows part of the thing that it represents.

Scientists also use computers to make models. You can watch on a computer screen how ocean conditions change over time. The model can show you how plant and animal populations are affected. You can even make a model using words. When you describe something, you are making a verbal model of the object. Other people can learn about the object from your spoken model.

Evaluate How could you make a model to explain how a lobster survives on the ocean floor?

_____

_____

_____

SEP.2 Developing and using models
SEP.6 Constructing explanations and designing solutions
SEP.7 Engaging in argument from evidence

Engaging in Arguments from Evidence

Scientific observations are different from opinions. An opinion is a personal belief and is not always based on facts. An example of an opinion is that tuna tastes better than salmon. No facts support this opinion. An example of a fact is that salmon lay their eggs in fresh water. This statement can be supported by observation.

Scientists use evidence to support their conclusions. For example, the conclusion that whales migrate is based on evidence. Whales can be seen in some areas but not in others, depending on the season. Scientists can also track individual whales to see where they go.

When a scientist makes a claim or argument, other scientists can check the evidence that the claim is based on. Different people making the same observation will find the same evidence. Scientific explanations are always based on empirical evidence.

Explain No one has seen a giant squid with a length of 20 meters. How could scientists use evidence to decide whether these animals exist?

_____

_____

_____

_____

_____

Science Practices

Habits of Mind

Scientists must be creative when they design experiments. Science is focused on answering new questions. That often means that scientists must come up with new ways to answer questions. Designing a good experiment requires them to think of new ways to solve problems. They need to think about what could go wrong and how to fix it. For example, a scientist who studies tiny organisms in the ocean might try to count them using a medical machine that counts blood cells.

When scientists develop new methods, they evaluate them to be certain they are collecting the right data to answer the question. After they have analyzed data and reached a conclusion, scientists share the results. Other scientists then review and evaluate the methods and conclusions. This peer review process helps confirm that investigations were correctly designed. Other scientists may also repeat the investigation to confirm that they obtain the same results.

Plan an Investigation Sea urchins eat a lot of kelp, an underwater organism. A scientist concludes that increasing populations of sea otters would help restore kelp forests because otters eat sea urchins. How could other scientists confirm this conclusion?

_____

_____

_____

_____

Communicate Information

Scientists communicate with other scientists to share what they learned. The words that scientists use sometimes have meanings different from the same word used in everyday communication. *Current,* *heat,* and *record* are examples of words that have a specific meaning in science. In science, for example, *heat*

Investigation Findings

Scientists around the world communicate and evaluate results.

refers to the flow of thermal energy. In everyday use, heat may refer to the temperature on a warm day.

Scientists do not perform a single observation or experiment and then come to a conclusion. They repeat experiments and gather the same kind of information. If the results cannot be repeated, then some of the observations may include errors. It is also important that scientific observations can be repeated by other researchers. Sometimes, other researchers cannot get the same result. Then the scientists compare their methods to find out what is different. An error could have happened in one of the methods.

Being able to repeat results makes a conclusion more reliable, so communication among scientists is important. Scientists communicate their methods and results, so other scientists can repeat them and then compare.

Evaluate A scientist repeats an experiment and gets a different result. What should the scientist do next?

_____

_____

_____

Engineering Practices

Defining Problems

Scientists study the natural world. Engineers apply scientific knowledge to solve problems. The first step of the engineering process is stating a well-defined problem. The engineering problem states exactly what the solution to the problem should accomplish. Engineers ask questions to define problems that need to be solved. For example, an engineer might want to build a probe to take samples very deep in the ocean. The engineer might start by asking "What kinds of tools can do that specific job?" Engineers use scientific knowledge and principles to solve the problem.

Before designing a solution, engineers identify criteria and constraints of the problem. The criteria are what the solution must accomplish. For example, one criterion when building a research submarine is that it must work well under the great pressure of the deep ocean. Constraints are limits on the solution. A constraint could be that a solution not go over a certain cost.

Evaluate A classmate says that the cost of an environmental project should not be considered a constraint. Do you agree? Why or why not?

_____

_____

_____

_____

SEP.1 Asking questions (for science) and defining problems (for engineering)
SEP.6 Constructing explanations (for science) and designing solutions (for engineering)
SEP.8 Obtaining, evaluating, and communicating information

Designing Solutions

Before designing a solution, engineers identify criteria and constraints of the problem. For example, one criterion of a solution to rebuild a harbor could be that it restores a habitat for certain animals. A constraint of the harbor restoration could be that it not cost too much money.

Engineers use the criteria and constraints to develop a solution to the problem. They may think of different ways to solve the engineering problem, then decide which way fits the criteria and constraints best.

After they decide on a solution, engineers build the solution and test it. They may use several different design ideas and evaluate each one. They often can combine the best features of each to come to a final design solution.

Design Solutions When ships release water from distant places, they can introduce invasive species. What kind of engineering solution would help prevent the spread of invasive species?

_____

_____

_____

_____

_____

_____

_____

Engineering Practices

Using Models and Prototypes

Similar to scientists, engineers frequently use models as they design solutions. Engineering models can be actual working devices of a proposed solution. Sometimes these devices represent the final solution, but perhaps on a smaller scale. They may only model one part of the solution. Other models are an actual device at full scale and perform all parts of the solution. This kind of model is called a prototype. Engineers use a prototype to collect data that can help them evaluate the design.

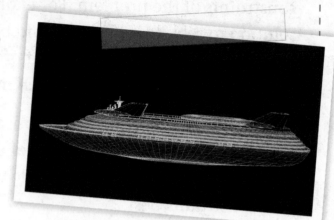

Engineers may use other kinds of models, such as drawings or computer models. A computer model can compare parts of a very complex solution. It allows engineers to make changes and observe what happens without investing a large amount of time or resources to actually build the solution. For example, an engineer investigating ways to restore a damaged ecosystem could use a computer to model changes to the system. The computer could model the effects of changes before the engineer decides which changes to make in a large area.

Infer Why would a computer model of a new ship design save time or money during the construction of the ship?

_____

_____

_____

SEP.2 Developing and using models
SEP.3 Planning and carrying out investigations
SEP.5 Using mathematics and computational thinking
SEP.7 Engaging in argument from evidence

Optimizing Solutions

Engineering is focused on solving problems. A successful solution must meet all of the criteria and constraints. Even if a solution is successful, a better solution may still be possible. When the design is tested, engineers may think of new ideas that might work. The criteria or constraints may also change during the process.

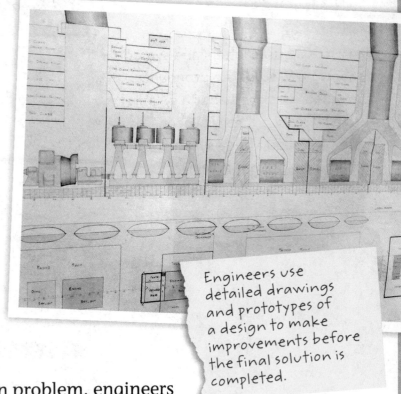

Engineers use detailed drawings and prototypes of a design to make improvements before the final solution is completed.

Even after solving the design problem, engineers continue to work on the solution to optimize it, or make it better. They evaluate the results and consider ways to improve on them. Then they may make a new prototype to determine whether it is a better solution. Like scientists, engineers make a change and then observe or measure the results of the change. After analyzing and evaluating their data, engineers may change the solution or develop a new engineering problem.

Optimize Solutions An engineer designs a project to restore a forest after a mining project. After the design is complete, more funding becomes available. How could the engineer optimize the design solution?

_____

_____

_____

_____

Glossary

The glossary uses letters and symbols to show how words are pronounced. The mark " is placed after a syllable with a primary or heavy accent. The mark ' is placed after a syllable with a secondary or light accent.

abiotic (ā′ bī ot″ ik) nonliving parts of an ecosystem

apparent (ə par″ ənt) how something looks

aquifer (ak″ wə fər) an underground water supply

atmosphere (at″ mə sfir) the layer of gases surrounding Earth

axis (ak″ sis) an imaginary line that goes through the center of an object

biosphere (bī″ ə sfir) the Earth system that includes all living things

biotic (bī ot″ ik) living parts of an ecosystem

carnivore (kär″ nə vôr) an animal that eats only other animals or products of other animals

chemical change (kem″ ə kəl chānj) a process in which a new kind of matter forms

chemical reaction (kem″ ə kəl rē ak″ shen) the process in which one or more substances change into one or more different substances

circulate (sėr″ kyə lāt) to move in a circle

classify (klas″ ə fī) to organize into groups based on a system

community (kə myü" nə tē) all organisms living in an ecosystem

competition (kom' pə tish" ən) when two or more organisms need the same limited resource to survive

component (kəm pō" nənt) a part

conclude (kən klüd") to make a statement with data and facts

condensation (kon' den sā" shən) the process in which a gas cools and becomes a liquid

conservation (kon' sər vā" shən) the protection and care of the environment and natural resources

conservation of matter (kon' sər vā" shən ov mat" ər) the scientific law that, in any physical or chemical change, the total mass of the matter does not change

constellation (kon' stə lā" shən) a group of stars that appear to make a shape or picture

consumer (kən sü" mər) an organism that needs to eat other organisms to survive

cycle (sī" kəl) to go through a series of events or processes that repeat

decomposer (dē' kəm pō" zər) an organism that breaks down the bodies of dead organisms

describe (di skrīb") to tell about the properties of an object

differentiate (dif' ə ren" shē āt) to identify the differences between two or more objects

distinguish (dis ting" gwish) to clearly show the differences between two objects

distribute (dis trib" yüt) to spread out

ecosystem (ē" kō sis' təm *or* ek" ō sis' təm) the living and nonliving things in an area

effect (ə fekt") a change caused by an action

efficient (ə fish" ənt) able to produce the effect wanted without wasting time or energy

establish (e stab" lish) to show an idea

evaporation (i va' pə rā" shən) the process in which a substance warms and changes from a liquid into a gas

exert (eg zèrt") to apply strength or effort

food chain (füd chān) a model that shows how matter and energy flow from one organism to another

food web (füd web) a model that shows the transfer of energy within a set of interconnected food chains

Glossary

gas (gas) matter that does not have a definite shape or volume

geosphere (jē" ō sfir') the Earth system that includes rocks, soil, sediments, and Earth's core and mantle

glacier (glā" shər) a slow moving body of ice on land

gravity (grav" ə tē) a force that pulls two objects together

greenhouse effect (grēn" hous' ə fekt") the process in which heat is trapped in Earth's atmosphere

herbivore (ėr" bə vôr or hėr" bə vôr) an animal that eats only plants

hydrosphere (hī" drə sfir) the Earth system that includes all water

interact (in' tər akt") to affect another organism and be affected by it

interdependent (in' tər di pen" dənt) a relationship where different parts depend on each other

liquid (lik" wid) matter with a definite volume but no definite shape

maintain (mān tān") to keep something in the same condition

mass (mas) the amount of matter in an object

measure (mezh" ər) to compare something to a standard unit

microbe (mī" krōb) an organism that is too small to see without a microscope

mineral (min" ər əl) a naturally occurring material

mixture (miks" chər) a substance where different materials are put together but each keeps its own properties

natural resource (nach" ər əl ri sôrs" or nach" ər əl rē" sôrs) a material found in nature that is used by humans

nonrenewable resource (non' ri nü" ə bəl ri sôrs" or non' ri nü" ə bəl rē" sôrs) a resource that is replenished at a slower rate than it is used

observe (əb zėrv") to use your senses to gather information

omnivore (om" nə vôr') an animal that eats both plants and other animals

orbit (ôr" bit) the curved path of an object around a star, a planet, or a moon

organize (ôr" gə nīz) to arrange something to make it easier to understand

pattern (pat" ərn) objects or events that occur in the same order or manner

physical change (fiz" ə kəl chānj) a change in some properties of matter that does not change what the substance is made of

pollution (pə lü" shən) harmful substances in the environment

precipitation (pri sip' ə tā" shən) water in the atmosphere that falls to Earth as rain, sleet, snow, or hail

primary (pri" mer' ē) the original or most important

producer (prə dü" sər) an organism that can make its own food using energy from the sun

related (ri lā" tid) connected

renewable resource (ri nü" ə bəl ri sôrs" or ri nü" ə bəl rē" sôrs) material made by nature at least as quickly as people use it

reservoir (rez" ər vwär) a place that holds water

revolution (rev' ə lü" shən) the movement of one object around another object

rock (rok) a natural material made from one or more minerals

rotation (rō tā" shən) the spinning of an object around its axis

salinity (sə lin" ə tē) the amount of salt dissolved in water

shadow (shad" ō) a dark area or shape made by an object or organism blocking a source of light

solid (sol" id) matter with a definite shape and volume

solubility (sol' yə bil" ə tē) how well a substance dissolves in another material

solution (sə lü" shən) a mixture in which the substances are evenly spread out and do not settle to the bottom of the container

Glossary

stable (stā" bəl) steady or unchanging

star (stär) a giant ball of hot, glowing matter

support (sə pôrt") to back up

system (sis" təm) a group of parts that work together to complete a task

temperature (tem" pər ə chər) a measure of how fast the particles of matter are moving

tide (tīd) a pattern of rising and falling water in the ocean caused by gravity

transfer (tran sfėr" *or* tran" sfėr′) to move from one object to another

volume (vol" yəm) the amount of space an object takes up

water cycle (wȯ" tər sī" kəl) the continuous movement of water on Earth

Index

* Page numbers for charts, graphs, maps, and pictures are printed in italics.

Index

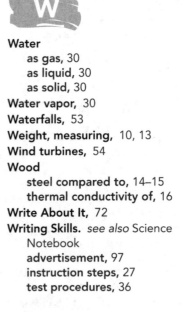

Photography

Photo locators denoted as follows: Top (T), Center (C), Bottom (B), Left (L), Right (R), Background (Bkgd)

Covers

Front: Bill Ross/Corbis/Getty Images; Back: Marinello/DigitalVision Vectors/Getty Images

Instructional Segment 1

iv: Nick Lundgren/Shutterstock; vi: Tim Oram/Oxford Scientific/Getty Images; vii: Milosz Maslanka/Shutterstock; viiiBkgd: Iakov Kalinin/Fotolia; viiiTR: Barry Tuck/Shutterstock; 000TL: Bayanova Svetlana/Shutterstock; 000TR: Sirtravelalot/Shutterstock; 003TL: Bayanova Svetlana/Shutterstock; 003TR: Sirtravelalot/Shutterstock; 004: Tim Oram/Oxford Scientific/Getty Images; 008: Number 76219/Shutterstock; 010: Brittany Nagle/PUSHLiving Photos; 010BL: Matt Grant/Shutterstock; 012: Oktay Ortakcioglu/E+/Getty Images; 013: Richard Megna/Fundamental Photographs; 016TL: Indianstockimages/Shutterstock; 017C: ESB Professional/Shutterstock; 017CR: Svetlana Foote/Shutterstock; 018: ESB Professional/Shutterstock; 019TR: Couperfield/Shutterstock; 019B: Syda Productions/Shutterstock; 020B: Qwzhu/Stockimo/Alamy Stock Photo; 020BR: Mark Baigent Life/Alamy Stock Photo; 024: Kinn Deacon/Alamy Stock Photo; 025T: ESB Professional/Shutterstock; 025BR: Alexeysun/Shutterstock; 026CL: Marcio Jose Sanchez/AP Images; 026BR: Marcio Jose Sanchez/AP Images; 026CR: Marcio Jose Sanchez/AP Images; 028: Mariusz Jurgielewicz/Alamy Stock Photo; 029BCR: Lineartestpilot/Shutterstock; 029BR: BeatWalk/Shutterstock; 031TR: Goss Images/Alamy Stock Photo; 031BR: Education Images/Universal Images Group North America LLC/Alamy Stock Photo; 032: ESB Professional/Shutterstock; 033TR: Dmitr1ch/Fotolia; 033CR: Aksenenko Olga/Shutterstock; 034T: ESB Professional/Shutterstock; 034BR: Viktor1/Shutterstock; 036: ESB Professional/Shutterstock; 037TR: Suwin/Shutterstock; 037B: SasinTipchai/Shutterstock; 040: Elina Li/Shutterstock; 042: Milosz Maslanka/Shutterstock; 044: Irmun/Shutterstock; 046: A and N photography/Shutterstock; 048: Antantarctic/Fotolia; 052B: Antonina Sotnykova/Shutterstock; 052CL: Tim UR/Shutterstock; 052BR: Aukarawatcyber/Shutterstock; 053: Donald Smith/Alamy Stock Photo; 053BC: A and N photography/Shutterstock; 055TL: A and N photography/Shutterstock; 055TR: Anne Gilbert/Alamy Stock Photo; 056: Cyran/Shutterstock; 058TL: Lersan Moomueansri/123RF; 058CR: A and N photography/Shutterstock; 059TR: David Taylor/Science Source; 059B: Nati Harnik/AP Images; 060B: Santiparp Wattanaporn/Shutterstsock; 060BL: Foto Images/Fotolia; 060CL: Kichigin/Shutterstock; 062TL: A and N photography/Shutterstock; 062B: Tibet Saisema/Shutterstock; 063B: Jeff Smith/Alamy Stock Photo; 063CR: Anne Cusack/Los Angeles Times/Getty Images; 064: Lukas Gojda/Fotolia; 065: Natasha Pankina/Shutterstock; 067C: galichstudio/Fotolia; 067CL: Galichstudio/Fotolia; 069TR: Mexrix/Shutterstock; 069BC: A and N photography/Shutterstock; 069CR: Ahavelaar/Fotolia; 072Bkgd: Mushy/Fotolia; 072BC: Magnago/Shutterstock; 072BCL: Ajt/Shutterstock; 072BL: Lizard/Shutterstock; 072BR: Daxiao Productions/Shutterstock; 073: Exopixel/Shutterstock; 073:

Steve Carroll/123RF; 074TR: A and N photography/Shutterstock; 074BCR: Scott Bolster/Shutterstock; 074BR: Pearson Education; 075: GlebTv/Shutterstock; 076C: Barry Tuck/Shutterstock; 076CL: RGtimeline/Shutterstock; 076BL: Dod/Fotolia; 076BR: Jay Beaumont/Fotolia; 078: Joannawnuk/Shutterstock; 080TL: Slava_Kovtun/Shutterstock; 080CL: Hemera Technologies/PhotoObjects.net/Getty Images Plus/Getty Images; 081B: Sergieiev/Shutterstock; 081BC: A and N photography/Shutterstock; 084: Richard Megna/Fundamental Photographs; 085: Donfiore/Shutterstock; 086Bkgd: Severija/Shutterstock; 086TC: A and N photography/Shutterstock; 088: Yatra/Shutterstock; 088: A and N photography/Shutterstock; 089TR: Javier Larrea/age fotostock/Getty Images; 089Bkgd: AshTproductions/Shutterstock; 093: Nine Homes/Shutterstock; 094TR: Africa Studio/Shutterstock; 094CR: Karamysh/Shutterstock; 096TC: Rob Byron/Shutterstock; 096TR: Alslutsky/Shutterstock; EM01: SergeUWPhoto/Shutterstock; EM02Bkgd: Don Paulson/Purestock/Alamy Stock Photo; EM02: Rattiya Thongdumhyu/Shutterstock; EM03: Suzanne Long/Alamy Stock Photo; EM05: National Oceanic and Atmospheric Administration (NOAA), U.S. Department of Commerce.; EM06: Fotosearch/Getty Images; EM07: M. Timothy O'Keefe/Alamy Stock Photo; EM09: Ariel Skelley/DigitalVision/Getty Images; EM11: CANARAN/Shutterstock; EM12: Vandrage Artist/Shutterstock; EM13: Stephen Barnes/Alamy Stock Photo.

My Notes and Designs

Draw, Write, Create

My Notes and Designs

Draw, Write, Create

My Notes and Designs

Draw, Write, Create

My Notes and Designs

Draw, Write, Create

My Notes and Designs

Draw, Write, Create

My Notes and Designs

Draw, Write, Create

My Notes and Designs

Draw, Write, Create